Academic English Communication for Graduate Students

研究生学术交流英语

主　编／李文梅

副主编／徐亚琴　王丽明

编　者／李　蓓　高　飞
　　　　官　濛

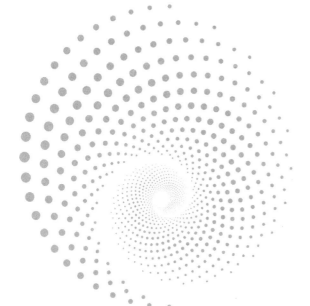

清华大学出版社
北　京

内 容 简 介

本教材全面覆盖研究生主要学术活动，包括：学术英语的内涵和特征；学术英语问题自我诊断及解决途径；文献获取、文献管理和文献综述的工具和方法；如何聆听学术报告；如何辨析国际会议信息；如何开展学术目的的英语通信和交谈；如何进行学术会议报告；如何进行学术目的的英语提问与回答；如何用英语主持学术会议；师生如何共建模拟国际学术大会等。每个单元由教学目标、课前问题、学术英语困难情景、翻转课堂、对分课堂、课后反思与实践、语言工具箱构成，实现了课前、课中和课后无缝衔接。

本教材可作为高等学校硕士生和博士生英语教材，也可供其他需要提高英语学术交流能力的人员使用。

版权所有，侵权必究。举报：010-62782989，beiqinquan@tup.tsinghua.edu.cn。

图书在版编目（CIP）数据

研究生学术交流英语 / 李文梅主编. —北京：清华大学出版社，2021.11
ISBN 978-7-302-58610-4

Ⅰ. ①研… Ⅱ. ①李… Ⅲ. ①学术交流—英语—研究生—教材 Ⅳ. ① G321.5

中国版本图书馆 CIP 数据核字（2021）第 131754 号

责任编辑：倪雅莉
封面设计：张伯阳
责任校对：王凤芝
责任印制：朱雨萌

出版发行：清华大学出版社
网　　址：http://www.tup.com.cn, http://www.wqbook.com
地　　址：北京清华大学学研大厦 A 座　　邮　编：100084
社 总 机：010-62770175　　邮　购：010-62786544
投稿与读者服务：010-62776969, c-service@tup.tsinghua.edu.cn
质量反馈：010-62772015, zhiliang@tup.tsinghua.edu.cn

印 装 者：大厂回族自治县彩虹印刷有限公司
经　　销：全国新华书店
开　　本：185mm×260mm　　印 张：17.5　　字 数：330 千字
版　　次：2021 年 11 月第 1 版　　印 次：2021 年 11 月第 1 次印刷
定　　价：75.00 元

产品编号：087134-01

前　言

　　研究生教育肩负着高层次人才培养和创新创造的重要使命，是国家发展、社会进步的重要基石，是应对全球人才竞争的基础布局。实现我国从研究生大国向研究生强国的跨越离不开研究生教育的改革、发展和创新；实现研究生教育质量的快速提升，教材建设是研究生教育质量的重要保证。本教材将知识传授、价值塑造和能力培养有机结合，在传授英语知识、专业知识和跨文化交际知识的基础上培养研究生的学术思辨、创新能力、专业沟通、合作能力和学术价值判断能力，助力他们建立正确的学术态度和立场，树立学术诚信和自信，养成坚韧的学术精神和强烈的科技强国情怀，勇于承担学术使命和攀登科研高峰，用英语顺利开展国际学术交流，建立中国学者形象。

　　本教材以研究生运用英语进行学术交流的深度和广度为依据，内容结合学术成长之旅，由逐步深入学术圈汲取学术营养，直到步入国际学术舞台开展学术对话，具有层层推进的递进性；倡导混合式教学思路，每单元有机融入微课和翻转教学元素，对分课堂开展基于问题的任务型、探究式、研讨式教学；"做中学"的理念贯穿教学始终，每单元设计课后实践活动，这些实践活动都是最后一单元的模拟国际大会的核心构件。教学中主张巧妙利用微课视频进行情境设计和问题设计，开展课前自主学习、课上研讨、课后团队合作，营造学术探究氛围和激发学术好奇心，倡导英语学术化和生活化的学习理念，课程内容紧扣学术生活，具有开放式和可扩展性，提供师生共同建构空间。

　　本教材主要分为四个模块：第一个模块为走近学术英语，通过设计课堂活动和任务帮助学生理解学术英语的内涵，引导学生诊断自身存在的学术英语技能薄弱之处，探讨提高学术英语口语的途径；第二个模块为步入学术圈，师生共同探究英语文献的获取、管理和综述工具及策略；第三个模块为初级学术英语交流，主要面向大多数研究生的学术英语需求，开始由学术英语的输入向输出过渡；第四个模块为高级学术英语交流，面向博士生国际会议交流，内容按照国际会议的流程展开，最终以师生共同建构模拟大会来展示研究生的国际化学术视野和跨文化交际能力。

　　需要注意的是，书中 Tasks 听力部分的音视频可以通过手机扫描对应二维码进行在线收听、收看或下载。其中 TED 演讲相关视频，在相应位置附有相关演讲者姓名及演讲题目。读者可上网访问 TED 官网 www.ted.com，在站内搜索对应视频进行在线收看。

研究生学术交流英语
ACADEMIC ENGLISH COMMUNICATION for Graduate Students

  本教材由多年来一直从事学术英语交流和国际学术会议交流教学的一线教师团队编著，是研究生综合英语改革项目的阶段性成果。教材的主要内容虽然在多轮教学实践中不断改进和更新，几易其稿，但仍难免存在疏漏和不当之处，恳请读者批评指正。

编者

2021 年 4 月

Contents

Part One Approaching Academic English

UNIT 1 Getting Acquainted with Academic English 3

1.1 Overall Impression of Academic English 4
    1.1.1 A Glance over Written Academic English 5
    1.1.2 A Glimpse of Spoken Academic English 7

1.2 Salient Features of Academic English 10
    1.2.1 Vocabulary 10
    1.2.2 Hedging 12

1.3 Differentiating Academic English & General English 15
    1.3.1 Main Features of Spoken Academic English 16
    1.3.2 Main Features of Written Academic English 20

UNIT 2 Cultivating Academic English Competencies 23

2.1 Diagnosing Your Academic English Language Competencies ... 24
    2.1.1 Identifying General Problems with Your Academic English Communication 25
    2.1.2 Understanding Specific Academic English Communication Language Abilities Scales 28
    2.1.3 Locating the Gap Between Your Language Abilities and the Standards 32

2.2 Ways to Improve Academic Communication Competencies ... 34
    2.2.1 Improving Academic Communication Language Abilities ... 34
    2.2.2 Enhancing Academic English Non-language Abilities 38

2.2.3　Grasping Essential Skills for Communication in the Main Oral Academic Scenarios 39

Part Two　Stepping into Academia

UNIT 3　Accessing Academic English Literature 45

3.1 Literature Sources and Types 46
　　3.1.1　Literature Sources 47
　　3.1.2　Major Literature Types 49

3.2 Retrieval Databases, Methods and Strategies 51
　　3.2.1　Retrieval Databases 51
　　3.2.2　Search Terms for Retrieval 54
　　3.2.3　Retrieving Methods 56
　　3.2.4　Retrieving Strategies 59

3.3 Tracking and Ordering Literature 61
　　3.3.1　Literature Tracking and Ordering Tools 62
　　3.3.2　Challenges and Precautions 64

UNIT 4　Managing Academic English Literature 67

4.1 Reference Management Tools 68
　　4.1.1　Some English Literature Management Tools 68
　　4.1.2　Main Features of English Literature Management Tools ... 69

4.2 Principles and Steps to Manage Academic English Documents ... 71
　　4.2.1　Following Some Principles to Manage Documents 71
　　4.2.2　Managing Documents in Pre-reading 72
　　4.2.3　Managing Documents in Preliminary Reading 73
　　4.2.4　Managing Documents in In-depth Reading 73
　　4.2.5　Managing Documents in Writing 74
　　4.2.6　Important Tips for Literature Management 75

UNIT 5 Reviewing Academic English Literature 79

- 5.1 Selecting Sources 80
  - 5.1.1 Reviewing Literature 81
  - 5.1.2 Evaluating Sources 84
- 5.2 Structuring a Literature Review 89
  - 5.2.1 Contents of a Literature Review 89
  - 5.2.2 Ways of Grouping a Literature Review 92
- 5.3 Citing Sources 94
  - 5.3.1 Plagiarism 95
  - 5.3.2 Summarizing, Paraphrasing and Direct Quotation 96
- 5.4 Following Academic Conventions in Referencing 101
  - 5.4.1 Styles of Referencing 101
  - 5.4.2 Verbs of Referencing 103

Part Three Basic Academic English Communication

UNIT 6 Sitting in English Academic Lectures 109

- 6.1 Be Active Listeners 110
  - 6.1.1 What Is Special of an Academic Lecture? 111
  - 6.1.2 Focusing on Language Use Strategy in Lectures 112
  - 6.1.3 Taking Notes 114
  - 6.1.4 Identifying Topic Sentences 117
- 6.2 Evaluating While Listening 120
- 6.3 Raising Questions for Further Understanding 125
  - 6.3.1 Functions of Asking Questions 125
  - 6.3.2 Purposes of Asking Questions 127

UNIT 7 Asking and Answering Academic Questions ... 131

- 7.1 Understanding Questions 132
  - 7.1.1 Reasons for Asking Questions 133
  - 7.1.2 Questioning in Q&A Session 133
- 7.2 Asking Questions 136
  - 7.2.1 Template of Asking a Question 136
  - 7.2.2 Types of Questions 138
- 7.3 Answering Questions 142
  - 7.3.1 General Skills for Answering Questions 143
  - 7.3.2 Direct Answers 145
  - 7.3.3 Avoidance 147

UNIT 8 Corresponding for Academic Purposes 155

- 8.1 Introduction of Academic Correspondence 156
  - 8.1.1 Definition of Academic Correspondence 156
  - 8.1.2 Various Purposes of English Academic Correspondence ... 157
- 8.2 Features of English Academic Correspondence 160
  - 8.2.1 Formats of Academic Correspondence 160
  - 8.2.2 Language Features of Academic Correspondence 164
- 8.3 Writing Strategies in Academic Correspondence 166
  - 8.3.1 Use You-attitude Rather Than I-attitude 166
  - 8.3.2 More Communicative Strategies in Correspondence 167

Part Four Advanced Academic English Communication

UNIT 9 Identifying International Conference Information 179

- 9.1 Benefits of Attending International Academic Conferences ... 180
- 9.2 Information Sources on International Academic Conferences ... 185

9.3 Varieties of Academic Conferences..187

9.4 Conference Information and Major Conference Activities....192

    9.4.1 Conference Information...193

    9.4.2 Major Conference Activities..195

UNIT 10 Making a Paper Presentation 199

10.1 Structuring a Presentation..200

    10.1.1 Opening..201

    10.1.2 Main Body 204

    10.1.3 Ending..205

10.2 Preparing a Presentation...208

    10.2.1 Preparation Procedure..209

    10.2.2 PowerPoint Design 212

10.3 Delivering a Presentation 215

    10.3.1 Presentation Skills..215

    10.3.2 Verbal Expressions...218

UNIT 11 Initiating Free Exchanges with Academics... 225

11.1 Preparing a Talk with Professionals.............................226

    11.1.1 Topic Choosing 227

    11.1.2 Information Collecting...227

    11.1.3 Idea Organizing and Outlining.......................................228

11.2 Starting a Talk with Professionals 230

    11.2.1 Talking with Familiar Professionals...............................230

    11.2.2 Talking with Strangers 231

11.3 Deepening the Topic 231

11.4 Shifting the Topic 233

UNIT 12 Presiding over a Session 235

12.1 Preparations Before the Session 236

12.2 Making an Opening Speech and Introducing a Speaker ...239

 12.2.1 Making an Opening Speech 240

 12.2.2 Introducing a Speaker 241

12.3 Q&A Sessions and Thank-You Speeches 244

UNIT 13 Co-constructing a Simulated International Conference 251

13.1 The Significance of Co-constructing a Simulated International Conference 252

 13.1.1 Distinguishing the Varieties of International Conferences 253

 13.1.2 Mastering the Whole Procedures of International Conferences 254

13.2 Major Sessions of Simulated International Conferences 255

 13.2.1 Organization of an International Conference 256

 13.2.2 Routine Work of Organizing an International Conference 256

13.3 How to Co-construct a Simulated International Conference 257

 13.3.1 To-do list at the Very Beginning of a Simulated International Conference 258

 13.3.2 Promoting a Simulated International Conference 259

 13.3.3 Calling for Paper of a Simulated International Conference 261

 13.3.4 Invitation Letter of a Simulated International Conference 262

 13.3.5 Agenda of a Simulated International Conference 262

13.4 The Evaluation of a Simulated International Conference 264

References 267

Part One

Approaching Academic English

UNIT 1
Getting Acquainted with Academic English

Learning Objectives

- To acquire a conceptual framework of academic English;

- To know main features of spoken academic English & written academic English;

- To develop your understanding of academic speaking and writing styles.

Pre-learning Questions

1. How much do you know about the differences between academic English and general English?
2. What differences are there between spoken academic English & written academic English?
3. In what way do the differences between oral mode and written mode affect writing and speaking styles?

In this unit, you will learn the concept of academic English (AE, hereafter). It is such a complicated concept that academics from different research areas provide various interpretations about it.

As a graduate student who just embarked on the scholarly journey, you must feel increasingly required to know what academic English means to you, its language features as well as expression patterns. This unit is designed to help you get your voices across to an international audience and thus make you a member of the academia at the global level. And at this age of globalization, you should strive to be a scholar with a world vision. Mastering AE will not only fulfill your graduation requirement, but also enable you to communicate smoothly in the academic circle. With the necessary knowledge, practical skills and beneficial suggestions provided in this unit, you can make a difference and make progress in academic English communication.

1.1 Overall Impression of Academic English

Classroom Voice

John, a first year graduate, who obtained an IELTS overall Level 7 in his undergraduate years, is confident in using English in everyday situations. Yet he finds the kind of English he is good at cannot satisfy the needs of his graduate studies, especially when reading English literature, presenting his ideas and writing academic essays. Therefore, he is eager to better his understanding of the type of academic English.

John feels puzzled about the questions: What is academic English characterized by? What is it used for?

UNIT 1 Getting Acquainted with Academic English

Instructor's Voice

Academic English, academic language in English, is also called English for Academic Purposes (EAP). AE is the type of English you need for:
- attending academic lectures;
- reading and understanding research literature;
- having a panel discussion;
- giving a scholarly presentation in a variety of situations;
- writing dissertations for a particular degree;
- publishing research papers;
- communicating with professionals about research projects…

If you read an article in an academic journal or listen to someone giving a presentation on an academic subject, AE is being used. If you are dealing with English for academic purposes, you surely need to learn this type of English. Native English speakers also have to learn AE because it is substantially different from the English that is used in daily life by English speakers.

1.1.1 A Glance over Written Academic English

Academic English falls into written mode and spoken mode. For a good knowledge of the former, you are suggested firstly to skim the following two abstracts of journal papers:

Abstract 1: (1) Rural household energy use for cooking and heating is an important source of air pollutants in China, as it affects both human health and climate change. (*Current situation*) (2) However, the magnitude of rural household energy use, especially during the recent rapid socioeconomic transition period, has not been well quantified. (*Research gap*) (3) In this paper, we presented first-hand nationwide data from a 34,489-household energy-mix survey and a 1,670-household fuel-weighing campaign. (*Method*) (4) We found that the consumption of wood and crop residues in rural China decreased by 63% and 51%, respectively, from 1992 to 2012, and these decreases were much greater than the 15% and 8%, respectively, reported by the International Energy Agency and Food and Agriculture Organization. (*Results*) (5) The rapid residential energy transition over these two decades was primarily driven by the rapid socioeconomic development. (*Conclusion*) (6) One important implication of this transition is the significant reduction in the emissions of major air pollutants, especially incomplete combustion products leading to significant impacts on health and climate. (*Conclusion*)

Abstract 2: (1) With a listening type writer, what an author says would be automatically recognized and displayed in front of him or her. However, speech recognition is not yet advanced enough to provide people with a reliable listening type writer. (***Background***) (2) An aim of our experiments was to determine if an imperfect listening typewriter would be useful for composing letters. (***Purpose***) (3) Participants dictated letters, either in isolated words or in consecutive word speech. They did this with simulations of listening typewriters that recognized either a limited vocabulary or an unlimited vocabulary. (***Method***) (4) Results indicated that some versions, even upon first using them, were at least as good as traditional methods of handwriting and dictating. (***Result***) (5) Isolated word speech with large vocabularies may provide the basis for a useful listening typewriter. (***Conclusion***)

In the above two abstracts you're expected to be able to see that…

(1) They use formal academic language and avoid colloquialisms.

The phrase "the magnitude of rural household energy use" really means "the amount of rural household energy use", but it uses more formal words.

(2) They are objective and impartial.

Being objective and impartial means that you have to prove everything you say and you do doesn't have bias before you start your research, or that you are stating a fact instead of an opinion. In the first abstract, specific figures and data are provided rather than using such ambiguous expressions as "a lot of" "some", etc.

(3) They are tentative and cautious.

Phrases like "would be useful for composing letters", and "Results indicated that…" are using hedging device to avoid arbitrariness. If you are not cautious, you might say something which later proves not to be true.

(4) There are signal words which create the discourse cohesion;

Here are some examples of "cohesive devices" such as "however" and "as".

(5) They present ideas or information in a logical, clear, structured way, which can be seen according to the numbered sentences.

As an essential part of an academic paper, an abstract is a miniature of the paper with a strictly limited number of words, which calls for being unified and coherent in content. Although an abstract can vary from research field to field, it may be not that difficult to see the discussed linguistic features, self-contained content and formalized structure in the two short abstracts.

Actually, the aforementioned abstracts are not meant to serve as, or cover fixed rules; however, it might be kind of useful guidance for your acquaintance with AE.

UNIT 1 Getting Acquainted with Academic English

> **Tasks**

Read the following extract of the Introduction Part in a journal article entitled "Chinese Voices: Chinese Learners and Their Experiences of Studying in the UK", and pay close attention to the writing style of the italicized parts by filling in the blanks with your own way of expressions.

Chinese students have an increasingly high profile in UK universities (1. <u>Formal and academic words are used here. Some students may write "There are more and more Chinese students..."</u>). In 2005 the number of Chinese students in UK universities was put at 50,000 (Higher Education Statistics Agency, 2007). According to Universities and Colleges Admissions Service (UCAS) (UCAS, 2008), *nearly 5,000 Chinese students were accepted to start courses at British universities* (2. _____) in autumn 2008, a rise of 14.7 percent on 2007. However, demographic changes in China and increasing competition from other parts of the globe offering higher education courses mean that *the number of students is expected to peak in 2011* (3. _____) (Gill, 2008). *As more institutions seek to attract a dwindling number of students we can expect greater competition* (4. _____) between universities and a resulting increase in the interest of the student experience. It is vital that institutions listen carefully to the experiences that their Chinese students are living through if they are to continue to attract students in the face of worldwide competition.

1.1.2 A Glimpse of Spoken Academic English

Academic English does not necessarily present itself in its written form. Spoken language serves for another manifestation of academic English, often in the form of giving a presentation, or a keynote speech, or having a panel discussion. But the language used in these situations is totally different from everyday English. Normally, similar to academic written English, academic spoken English is also precise, clear, concise, cautious, and formal. In other words, spoken language, to achieve clarity and formality, mainly abides by the principles of "talking to you" "choosing the right words" "speaking simple language" "employing hedging device" "avoiding zeroes without information", etc.

Tasks

1 Listen to the beginning and ending of the speech. What typical characteristics can you see from this type of academic English compared with everyday spoken English? Discuss with your group members and then report your findings to the class.

Half of the human workforce is expected to be replaced by software and robots in the next 20 years. And many corporate leaders welcome that as a chance to increase profits. Machines are more efficient; humans are complicated and difficult to manage.

Well, I want our organizations to remain human. In fact, I want them to become beautiful. Because as machines take our jobs and do them more efficiently, soon the only work left for us humans will be the kind of work that must be done beautifully rather than efficiently.

To maintain our humanity in this second Machine Age, we may have no other choice than to create beauty. Beauty is an elusive concept. For the writer Stendhal it was the promise of happiness. For me it's a goal by Lionel Messi.

So bear with me as I am proposing four admittedly very subjective principles that you can use to build a beautiful organization.

First: do the unnecessary.

A few months ago, Hamdi Ulukaya, the CEO and founder of the yogurt company Chobani, made headlines when he decided to grant stock to all of his 2,000 employees. Some called it a PR stunt, others—a genuine act of giving back. But there is something else that was remarkable about it. It came completely out of the blue. There had been no market or stakeholder pressure, and employees were so surprised that they burst into tears when they heard the news. Actions like Ulukaya's are beautiful because they catch us off guard. They create something out of nothing because they're completely unnecessary.

...

The second principle: create intimacy.

...

So to do the unnecessary, to create intimacy, to be ugly, to remain incomplete—these are not only the qualities of beautiful organizations, these are inherently human characteristics. And these are also the qualities of what we call home. And as we disrupt, and are disrupted, the least we can do is to ensure that we still feel at home in our organizations, and that we use our organizations to create that feeling for others.

UNIT 1 Getting Acquainted with Academic English

Beauty can save the world when we embrace these principles and design for them. In the face of artificial intelligence and machine learning, we need a new radical humanism. We must acquire and promote a new aesthetic and sentimental education. Because if we don't, we might end up feeling like aliens in organizations and societies that are full of smart machines that have no appreciation whatsoever for the unnecessary, the intimate, the incomplete and definitely not for the ugly.

Thank you.

(Source: Tim Leberecht's TED Talk entitled "Can AI Take Our Jobs?")

❷ Revise the following sentences for conciseness.

1. On previous occasions we have worked together.
2. He is a person who works hard.
3. We have completely eliminated the bugs from this program.
4. The purpose of this report is to update our research findings.

❯ Language Toolkit

Language Preferences for Formal Style and Informal Style:

Formal	Informal
Avoid colloquialism; use literary forms (e.g. claim, wonderful, many, however, therefore)	May use colloquial words and expressions (e.g. say, awesome, a lot, but, so)
Prefer single-word verbs (e.g. examine, increase, fluctuate, reduce, acquire)	May use multi-word verbs (e.g. look into, go up, go up and down, cut down, get hold of)
Avoid contractions; write out full words (e.g. cannot, will not, should not)	May use contractions (e.g. can't, won't, shouldn't)
More often write in third person	May use first, second, third person
Avoid using "you"; use "one" or "the reader"	May use "you" to address readers
Avoid questions; use declarative sentences (e.g. One may wonder at the question…)	May ask questions (e.g. Do you know…?)
May prefer passive voice sometimes (e.g. It has been found that…)	Often use active voice (e.g. I found that…)

> **Reflection & Practice**

1. Why is it essential for graduate students to have a good command of academic English?
2. Read at least 3 papers from the top journals in your research field to check whether the features mentioned in this section are applicable in these academic paper and exchange your observations with your desk-mates.
3. Watch at least five TED presentations on academic topics to analyze what kind of obstacles prevent you from following them and come up with the corresponding countermeasures.

1.2 Salient Features of Academic English

Classroom Voice

Lily thinks that she is now able to articulate her idea, both for academic speaking and writing purposes, in a more efficient way after she has learned the features of academic English discussed above. However, she experienced setbacks, because the presentation she made was regarded as subjective and unsupported. In addition, her paper writing was rejected by her supervisor. Thus, Lily got increasingly frustrated.

Instructor's Voice

Have you ever thought about the question: "What matters to academic English?" Your answer to this question somehow determines whether you are able to go directly to academic English in an appropriate way. For the sake of communication, academic English cannot work as it is without the adequate manifestation of academic English features including diction, hedging, and content, which encompasses the development of idea, how the line of thought is organized, and the exchange of ideas is conducted in a wide range of academic settings.

1.2.1 Vocabulary

Academic English is characterized by its numerous technical terms, specific content words and a large number of foreign words.

1) Technical Terms

The terms or words used in academic situations are typically professionalized. Let's take the word "normal" as an example. Generally, it means "正常的"; but as a mathematical term, it means

"法线"; and in the field of chemistry, it is "当量". Again the word "power", in electronics, it is rendered as "电源", in mechanics, "动力"; whereas in mathematics, it is translated as "幂".

Even in the same field, the meanings of a word may vary slightly due to its different collocations, for example:

> filter 滤波器，滤色器　　air filter 空气过滤器　　tramp filter 干扰滤除器
> amplitude filter 振幅滤波器　　filter paper 滤纸　　primary filter 基色滤色器

What is more, a great number of professional words and terms can only be understood by specialists in the fields, e.g. decoder (译码器), photophor (磷光核), multi-quantum transition (多量子跃迁), conversational implicatures (会话含义), etc. Examples like these are too numerous to list one by one. It can be of help to establish the clear awareness of this lexical feature in academic communication.

2) Specific Content Words

In English, it is not uncommon to see verb phrases made up of "verb + adv. / prep.", but these verb phrases often have more than one meaning. So their meanings are sometimes not easy to determine. In these cases, we often replace a verbal phrase by a single word of a specific meaning. For instance, we use "absorb" to replace "take in" or "take up", and "discover" to substitute for "find out", for these single verbs have more specific and accurate meanings, and appear much more formal and effective in creating an academic atmosphere. Again, the verb "observe" is more specific and accurate than the phrase "look at" in expressing the professional concept of "观察". Thus, making good use of this feature will be beneficial for writing and speaking accurate and concise English.

3) Foreign Words

Many English words of Greek, Latin and French origin are still used as part of Academic English vocabulary, especially in scientific and technical terminology. Words like "acupuncture" (针灸), "ambulance" (救护车), "amnesia" (健忘), "stimulus" (刺激物), "focus" (焦点), from Latin; and "technology" (工艺), "acrylic" (丙烯酸), "acoustics" (声学), "aerodynamics" (空气动力学), "agronomy" (农艺学) from Greek; "chiffon" (雪纺), "bureau" (办公桌) from French... They are presumably not that clear to English language learners, even to English native speakers. It is also a fact that both Greek and Latin words are used as affixes from which quite a few words can be derived. Derivative morphemes, including prefixes such as micro-, auto-, multi-, and suffixes as -logy, -ion, -graph, etc. can be found in academic papers. Hence, if you get familiar with this feature of word-formation, it will help enlarge your English vocabulary and improve your academic level. The following diagram shows the word building of professional vocabulary.

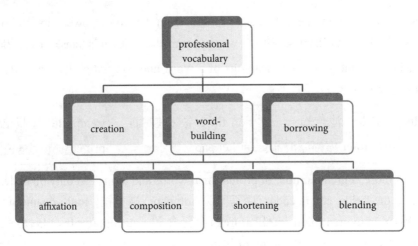

Figure 1.1　Source of Professional Vocabulary

1.2.2 Hedging

It is the expression of tentativeness and possibility. It is a unique art in academic communication, where making claim to knowledge at a proper level is essential. The cautiousness is called hedging. Chances are that in your writing or presentation there may be information or evidence that you have not found and that are exceptions to the conclusion that you have drawn. In this case you need to use hedge language to avoid the possibility of people saying you are not wrong, or to minimize or soften what you say.

Hedging purposes in scientific articles are categorized by Hyland (1996), as reproduced below with Hyland's examples:

Table 1.1　Categorization of Scientific Hedges

Category	Examples
1. Content-oriented hedges (including **accuracy-oriented hedges** and **writer-oriented hedges**) **Accuracy-oriented hedges**: Proposition-focused and seek to increase precision by referring to the exact state of knowledge or to how a proposition is to be understood.	a. Attribute hedges allow the writer to specify more precisely the attributes of the phenomena described. e.g. This shift could be <u>partially</u> caused by solvent-exposed α-helical segments of its coiled-coil portion. b. Reliability hedges indicate the writer's confidence in the truth of a proposition. e.g. However, the opposite is also possible, and it <u>cannot be ruled out that</u>…

(cont.)

Category	Examples
Writer-oriented hedges: Writer-focused and aimed at shielding the writer from the consequences of opposition by limiting personal commitment.	e.g. • Although it is premature to answer this question it might be suggested that… • This hypothesis seems plausible because… may…
2. Reader-oriented hedges Typically use person pronouns for expression of personal belief, and verbs of judgment and deduction, to weaken claims. Questions may also serve as hedges, since they appeal to the reader as a fellow scientist engaged in the scientific quest.	e.g. • Our interpretation of these results is that… • Under these conditions, we predicted that seedlings would… • Could such a…have a physiological significance?

In a research paper, hedging is characteristic of the sections of Introduction and the Discussion, while other sections such as Methods and Results avoid hedging. Many of us find it challenging to write the Introduction and the Discussion of a paper. In fact, proper use of hedging in the two sections is partly responsible for our success or failure in the two sections. Likewise, hedging is used in academic speaking.

Tasks

❶ Read the extract of Introduction Part from an essay entitled "The 'Fish-hook' Phenomenon in Centrifugal Separation of Fine Particle" before you discuss with your group members about how the author developed his ideas by using the underlined language.

Many people (Luckie & Austin, 1974; Finch, 1983; Del Villar & Finch, 1992; Patil & Rao, 2001) have assumed that the recovery of ultrafine particles in a hydrocyclone underflow increases with decrease in particle size beyond a critical particle size, known as "fishhook" effect. This critical particle size varies with the nature and characteristics of particles to be classified. But none could explain whether this irregular behavior with ultrafine particle sizes in a hydrocyclone is a characteristic phenomenon or not. It is also interesting to note that none could give any indication whether the similar fish-hook effect will be observed while processing ultrafine particles in any centrifugal force field.

Therefore, an attempt has been made to develop general understanding of the migration behavior of fine and ultrafine particles in a centrifugal force field.

❷ Read the extract of Discussion Part in a professional paper and underline its hedging devices.

Much of our data can be explained in the context of forest succession and known disease patterns. Clearly, sporadic insect out-breaks and climatic events have caused excessive mortality of certain species in certain stands. Some stands exhibited mortality as high as 40 %. However, an average of 20 % dead stems in a stand appears to be reasonable without inferring excessive mortality or decline.

Decline symptoms were not evident for the major canopy dominants. Living stems of both Quercus spp and Carya spp appeared healthy. However, these two groups had reasonably high mortality (16%-17%). Whether these mortality patterns are inordinately "high" or just "average" for mature, second-growth oak-hickory vegetation is not particularly clear.

Several studies have taken a populational approach to the examination of declining health of Ohio's forest species. McClenahen and McCarthy (1990) determined that a significant decrease in crown vigor of Pinusrigida could be due to air pollution in the Ohio valley. Likewise a similar study indicated a possible connection between pollution and altered patterns in white oak (McClenahen & Dochinger 1985). These and other studies indicate pollution as a possible factor in decline (but) as these authors acknowledge, absolute linkage between cause and effect is often very difficult to prove. Nash et al. (1992) encountered a similar problem in examining the health of oak-hickory vegetation in central Pennsylvania.

❯ Language Toolkit

Hedging Categories and Useful Expressions for Academic English:

Table 1.2 Hedging Expressions

Category	Examples
Certain introductory verbs and phrases	to tend, to look like, to appear to be, to think, to believe, to seem, to our knowledge, it is our view, we feel that
Certain modal lexical verbs	to assume, to suggest, to indicate, to estimate
Certain modal auxiliary verbs	could, can, will, would, may, might
Certain adverbs of frequency & degree	generally, normally, often, sometimes, usually, approximately, roughly, about, occasionally, somewhat, somehow, rarely, frequently

(cont.)

Category	Examples
Certain modal verbs & adjectives	probably, possibly, conceivably, possible, probable, (un)likely, presumably, virtually, apparently, arguably
Certain modal nouns	assumption, possibility, probability, claim, estimate, suggestion
Certain clauses introduced by it	It is possible / probable to obtain, It could be the case that, It might be suggested that, There is every hope that, It is important to develop, It is useful to study
Certain expressions of quantity	little, few, less, many, a number of, some, a lot of

⟩ Reflection & Practice

1. What are the biggest difficulties you have encountered when you started to read the Academic English literature?

2. What kind of technical terms in your research direction are frequently used in academic English papers?

3. Examine the use of hedging in Discussion Section of 10 most cited papers from the international top journals in your field and conduct a statistical survey of the most frequent hedges used there.

1.3 Differentiating Academic English & General English

Classroom Voice

Jennifer is increasingly aware of the differences between what is known as "academic English" and "general English", particularly those between academic presentation and everyday spoken English. For example, she knows that academic English may be used to either describe an object and situation or explain something. Nevertheless, as she moves on in her research area, she deems it difficult to use a language style appropriate to her subject, purpose and audience, and to communicate information, ideas and arguments effectively.

In the academic circle, she finds it seems far from what she thinks. Academic communication in English is really demanding.

Instructor's Voice

Jennifer's puzzle is associated with several problems: whether she can master academic English language (language ability); whether her knowledge and critical understanding of her subject shows its scope and depth, including some specialist areas (intellectual structure); and on the basis of that, whether she can synthesize, evaluate and challenge information from different sources (analytical ability), etc.

Apart from Jennifer's knowledge, much of academic English is about describing how things work, and expressing the relationship between ideas. Although the language may be more complex than everyday English, good academic writers aim to be as clear, precise, formal but simple as possible. They think about what their readers have known, and intend to guide them towards less familiar areas and topics. Therefore, it is important that you are proficient in English language. Moreover, it is equally important to structure and organize the presentation and a piece of writing by distinguishing features between academic English and general English, on which this unit will focus.

1.3.1 Main Features of Spoken Academic English

The ability to give an academic talk and to write in an academic style is something you develop as part of your postgraduate study. The premise is that you understand the field of your presentation or writing relatively well. On top of that, viewed from the angle of language, it is difficult to give overall "rules" on the way to write for an academic course, as academic subjects vary in:

- their vocabulary and expressions;
- the types of text used (for instance essays, reports, research articles or summaries);
- the way these texts are structured and organized.

The language style used in speaking (e.g. an oral presentation) is totally different from that used in an essay. A presentation with the variety of words and structure will be good for readers but harder for audience. The audience usually have no chance to ask the speaker to repeat or explain to them if they miss a certain point simply because you use different wording.

What matters to spoken academic English, used frequently in the academic talks, is that it is an oral one, not a written one. This may seem a self-evident statement, but you would be surprised at the fact that numerous speakers, including experts in some fields, simply write down their remarks and then report the speech verbatim to the audience. This can cause problems, for the act of reading is very different from that of listening. Here come some tips for making academic presentations in an appropriate style, for helping distinguish academic spoken English from everyday English:

UNIT 1 Getting Acquainted with Academic English

- It is not a casual conversation, so a very informal speaking style is not appropriate.
- It is spoken, not written, so reading aloud a typical written academic text is not appropriate.
- An appropriate academic speaking style falls between the two extremes, as it is shown below:

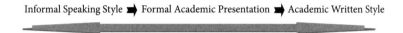

Figure 1.2 Progressive Relation Between Styles

The following three sentences vary in style:

Sentence 1:

It appears that in a number of instances jobs were assigned on the basis of gender. Given the current anti-discrimination laws, this raises serious concerns. (formal writing style)

Sentence 2:

Obviously, people got jobs just because they were men or women. I don't think it is OK and is even against the law. (typical speaking style)

Sentence 3:

It's so obvious that people were employed just because of gender difference. The approach is unreasonable and actually goes against the law. (more formal speaking style)

The above three sentences show it is not easy to move through flexibly different language styles between academic English and general English, between spoken academic English and written academic English. But the following **principles** will facilitate your distinctions between various types of English. Different language styles vary mainly in: (1) objectivity; (2) clarity; (3) simplicity; (4) complexity; (5) formality; (6) repetition, etc.

Compare the changes in this sentence from informal style to academic style:

Example 1:

When I look at the situation in emergency wards, with many staff leaving, it's hard not to worry about how many doctors will be available to treat patients in the future. (informal style)

If we consider the situation in emergency wards, with increasingly low staff retention rates, there are concerns about the capacity of hospitals to maintain adequate to patient ratios. (academic style)

Example 2:

It's so obvious that people were given jobs just because they were male or female. I don't think that it is an acceptable approach and is even against the law. (informal style)

It appears that in a number of instances jobs were assigned on the basis of gender. Given the current anti-discrimination laws, this raises serious concerns. (academic style)

Normally, academic style aims to be objective in its expression of ideas. Therefore specific references to personal opinions, or to yourself as the performer of some actions, are usually avoided.

In academic talks we use formal language, avoiding the use of slang and colloquial language. For example, what are language styles of the following four sentences respectively? Which express similar meanings?

A. Lots of people don't have enough money to get food.

B. Many people don't have enough money to buy food.

C. Poverty and hunger are widespread.

D. Many people do not have sufficient money to purchase food.

Compare the four sentences, you will find: A is the least formal; B is more formal than A; C is more formal than B, which is typical of academic speaking and writing, short, clear with abstract nouns; D is more formal than B, using elaborate vocabulary but without precise information. The entire presentation in the style of D would sound heavy and pompous.

❯ Tasks

❶ Read the following sentences to tell the writing style from the speaking style.

A. Home quarantine changed the face of the once bustling city.

B. The city had once been peaceful, but it changed when people got to be quarantined home.

A. The people in the colony rejoiced when it was promised that things would change in this way.

B. Public opinion in the colony greeted the promised change with enthusiasm.

❷ Read the following excerpt from TED talks on active evolution, and answer the questions below.

1. What are the transitional words the speaker used when he turned from one point to another?

2. What are the colloquial expressions the speaker used? Why did the speaker use them?

3. In which aspects does the talk differ from a formal essay?

UNIT 1 Getting Acquainted with Academic English

Hello everyone. Welcome to this evening.

If I can just have a bit of light on the audience so I'm seeing people and not darkness. Thanks.

What I want to talk to you today is about the next big revolution in history. A revolution which will occur during our lifetime. Actually, it's beginning already today or in the last few years. Now throughout history there are many different revolutions, the revolution in economics, in society, in politics, in technology. But one thing always remained constant throughout history for thousands of years and this is humanity itself.

We are still the same humans that we were in the time of Confucius or in the time of the pyramids or of the Bible or even in the time of the Stone Age. We still have the same bodies, the same brains, the same minds that we had ten or twenty or thirty thousand years ago. This has been the great constant of history. However, as we look to the future to the next few decades, what we are likely to see is of course many more revolutions in economics, in technology, in politics, and so forth. But above all, we are likely to seem a major revolution in humanity itself.

For the first time in history, we will change not just the world outside us but above all, we will change the world inside us. For thousands of years, humans have learned how to control and manipulate the world outside us, but they could not control what was happening inside themselves. We knew for example if a river was flowing, we knew how to build a dam and stop the river from flowing. But we did not know how to stop the body from ageing, the river of time of age. We did not know how to stop or reverse that.

Similarly, if you went to sleep at night and a mosquito starting buzzing in your ear and interrupting your sleep, people knew how to kill the mosquitos, how to drain the swamps and kill all the mosquitos. But if you went to sleep at night and a thought began buzzing in your mind, disturbing your sleep, we did not know what to do about that. We have no control over thoughts in the same way we have control over the mosquitos.

…

Thank you. (Applause)

(Source: Yuval Noah Harari's TED Talk entitled "What Explains the Rise of Humans")

〉Language Toolkit

Avoiding too many references to yourself as the agent in your presentation is recommended as shown in the following right column.

With agent or performer	Without agent or performer
I undertook the study… I propose to… In this paper I will examine…	The study was undertaken…

> **Reflection & Practice**

1. What do the **principles** (in Page 17) in academic speaking style and academic writing style imply?
2. Try to apply the principles mentioned to make a presentation on the topic in your field.

1.3.2 Main Features of Written Academic English

Classroom Voice

Li Tao can speak English well enough for daily life: shopping, travelling and meeting people. But he is surprised to find that writing essays and reports in English is a different case, much more difficult, especially when he was encouraged to write essays for publication. He does not know what to do, and becomes anxious. Having browsed a quantity of professional papers in his field recommended by his supervisor, he realized that it might be helpful to think about the way words are used in written language.

Why is writing English more difficult than speaking? What kind of language style is it in academic written English? What does a good professional writing feature?

Instructor's Voice

The features of academic writing are too many to numerate. Several elements contribute to the reason why writers have trouble in writing. First, speaking is usually done face to face. If your listener cannot understand you, they can look puzzled and ask you to repeat. But this does not work with a reader! When we write, we usually have little idea who may read our work, so we have to write as clearly as possible so that it is easy to understand. In writing, language is the way that words are used. Language is word choice, the arrangement of phrases, the structuring of sentences and paragraphs, and more. In academic written language, one of the major considerations is language style. Li Tao's questions prompt us to think about academic English in depth.

Whether you are a writer or a reader, it is quite necessary for you to put yourself in the benefit of others. The purpose is to get both you and your audience involved in a dialogue with the ideas obtained from your writing. Taking this into consideration, you will know how to communicate with your readers by writing in an effective way. For instance, with academic writing, writers and readers have to learn special conventions, such as using capital letters in certain places. If you do not follow these conventions, your meaning may be unclear and your reader might have difficulty understand your work.

One major problem is that many papers are poorly written. Some scientists are poor writers. Many others do not enjoy writing, and do not take the time or effort to ensure that the prose is clear and logical. Also, the author is typically so familiar with the material that it is difficult to step back and see it from the point of view of a reader not familiar with the topic and for whom the paper is just another large stack of papers that need to be read.

As its objective is to inform rather than entertain, an academic essay is characterized by objectivity and preciseness. To achieve the purposes, formality is an important element of a research project. A scholarly vocabulary and a consistently serious tone are representative of formal style. Nonetheless, formality does not contradict with preciseness.

Although there is no fixed standard of academic writing, it is clearly different from the writing style of newspapers or novels. For example, it is generally agreed that academic writing attempts to be accurate and objective.

Authors of similar course books provide a variety of features of professional writing for their readers' reference. On the one hand, it is somehow a guide; on the other hand, it is presumably misleading their readers. For example, with regard to the use of person, some books tell the students to avoid the first person (e.g. "I", "we", etc.) in academic writing. On the contrary, some others suggest the students use the first person. Accordingly, readers are likely to be confused. The key here is that we develop our critical thinking.

〉 Tasks

Read the the following explanations, and then write two simple and two longer sentences using data from the table below.

Table 1.3   Chinese Enterprises—Face Masks Production 2019–2020

Year	2016	2017	2018	2019	Up to May, 2020
Production	3 billion	2.87 billion	4.54 billion	5 billion	7 billion

All the following sentences contain verbs:

In 2019, the companies **produced** over 5 billion masks.

Between 2019 and 2020, masks production will **increase** by 20 percent.

Simple sentences (above) are easier to write and read, but longer sentences are prevalent in academic writing. However, students should make clarity a priority, and avoid writing very lengthy sentences with several clauses until they feel confident in their ability.

Sentences containing two or more clauses use conjunctions, relative pronouns or punctuation to link the clauses:

In 2019, the companies produced over 5 billion masks, **but** the following year production increased by 10 percent. (conjunction)

In the half of 2020, the companies will produce 16 billion masks, **which** is the expected peak of production. (relative pronoun)

Nearly 3 billion masks were produced in 2016**;** by 2017, this had fallen to 2.87 billion. (punctuation)

Your sentences:

1. _____

2. _____

3. _____

4. _____

❯ Language Toolkit

Useful Sentence Patterns of Writing Research Purpose of Paper:

- This problem is concerned (deals)(chiefly, largely, and mainly) with…
- This is a problem relating to…
- Our work is devoted to…
- The primary goal of the present research is…
- The chief aim of this study is…
- The laboratory study demonstrates (suggests, indicates, reveals, establishes)…
- Doing this work, we intend (hope, expect, attempt) to…
- The work presented in this paper focuses on several aspects of…

❯ Reflection & Practice

1. Interview your group members and one expert who have a wealth of experience in paper writing, and ask the following questions: What difficulties do they have in their writing? How do they solve their problems?

2. Work in groups to share other features of academic written English that may be elaborated.

UNIT 2
Cultivating Academic English Competencies

Learning Objectives

- To learn what academic English competencies are composed of;

- To locate the academic competency gap with comparison to the Standards;

- To describe and discuss the possible cultivation paths;

- To develop academic mindset and increase academic communication and dissemination awareness.

Pre-learning Questions

1. What are your strengths and weaknesses in academic English?
2. What is your understanding of academic English competencies?
3. What might be the problems in improving your academic English competencies?

In this unit, you will learn from general to specific what academic English language competencies are, mainly for oral and aural academic communication. Taking a problem-solution approach, you're expected via accomplishing an academic competence survey to find out the problems hard for you to conquer and the gap for you to bridge so as to reach a goal of effective academic communication in the main academic English scenarios. You will also learn and practise how to improve your academic value judgement, academic innovation ability, as well as your academic language abilities and academic communication strategies to prepare yourself for the further study.

2.1 Diagnosing Your Academic English Language Competencies

Classroom Voice

Richard, since he has just started his graduate study in his first year, can feel clearly there is a lot ahead for him to learn about academic English. Though he has known the difference between general English and academic English, he still has no idea that with what academic English competencies he can have a better performance in his academic communication.

Richard also feels confused, though he knows the competence scales, yet he has a vague idea of how far he is from the academic English ability goal. He decides to make it clear what problems he needs to solve in attaining his academic English communication abilities.

Instructor's Voice

To cultivate academic communication abilities, you need to find out what confusion you have about academic English communication competencies and what specific problems you have in improving academic English abilities. Describe the same confusion if you have as Richard does, and offer your suggestion for Richard to locate the gap between his English level and the standard of academic English competencies so as to make a plan to improve the ability.

UNIT 2 Cultivating Academic English Competencies

Where there is a goal, there is power. According to China's Standards of English Language Ability (CSE), users with advanced listening comprehension, oral language expression, pragmatic ability, linguistic knowledge and language use strategies, are required to understand language materials on topics related to his or her field of specialization or discuss familiar topics in academic interactions. This section provides and explains the speaking and listening language competencies for academic communication purpose. Focus your attention on the academic requirements and the academic contexts. It is hoped that students like you and Richard will have a good understanding of the academic communication at the end of this section.

2.1.1 Identifying General Problems with Your Academic English Communication

With a good knowledge of the distinctive features of academic English, students are suggested to evaluate their academic language competencies by referring to the overall academic English requirements of CSE.

1) Overall Academic Language Abilities

Though communication involves both oral and written modes, language abilities here will mainly cover the voice communication.

2) Overall Listening Comprehension Academic Abilities

Listening comprehension ability, as a comprehensive cognitive competence of listening, comprises the competence of identification, extraction, summary, analysis, critique and assessment. Students are expected to understand (highly-informative) academic spoken discourses (e.g. lectures, presentations, discussions) related to his/her own field and comprehend the main ideas and supporting details, and identify speakers' organizational patterns (e.g. overall framework, use of cohesive devices).

3) Overall Oral Expression Academic Abilities

Speakers with good oral expression academic abilities can express his/her viewpoints accurately and fluently on professional topics at academic seminars, can make formal academic presentations and provide further explanation based on questions, using accurate, clear, and coherent language, and can discuss about hot social issues or familiar topics in his/her field and respond appropriately to remarks, interruptions, etc.

> **Tasks**

❶ To get well-prepared for a better performance in the academic scenarios, you are suggested to do listening of academic speeches regularly from some public academic resources. You may take notes of both the outline and the main details.

A three-level outline is recommended as follows:
1. Topic/Theme: _____
2. Main Ideas: _____
_____
_____

3. Sub-ideas: _____
_____
_____

Tips: For the details, you may choose to write down either the important details of the speeches or those examples you are interested in.
Important details: _____
_____
_____

❷ A faster and more effective way of knowing your problems might be taking a survey on Academic English Communication Competencies based on the CSE listening comprehension, oral expression academic abilities and organizational competence. Take a survey on Academic Communication English Competencies, and briefly describe the survey based on the following model.

Background of the survey: _____
Respondents of the survey: _____
Purpose of the survey: _____
Result of the survey: _____
Analysis of the survey: _____
Conclusions of the survey: _____

UNIT **2** Cultivating Academic English Competencies

A Survey on Your Academic English Competencies			
Description of EAP Competencies		**Self-assessment**	**Solutions**
Overall Listening Comprehen-sion Academic Abilities	You can understand (highly-informative) academic spoken discourses (e.g. lectures, presentations, discussions) related to your own field and comprehend the main ideas and supporting details, and identify speakers' organizational patterns (e.g. overall framework, use of cohesive devices).		
Overall Oral Expression Academic Abilities	You can express your viewpoints accurately and fluently on professional topics at academic seminars, can make formal academic presentations and provide further explanation based on questions, using accurate, clear, and coherent language, and can discuss about hot social issues or familiar topics in your field and respond appropriately to remarks, interruptions, etc.		
Academic Organiza-tional Competence	-Grammatical Competence: You can accurately-naturally use the grammatical knowledge in English oral communication. -Vocabulary Competence: You can apply (common) academic and professional vocabulary;can understand and use appropriately in listening and speaking the complex profession-specific grammatical forms, including nominalization in the contexts of science and technology.		

(cont.)

A Survey on Your Academic English Competencies				
Description of EAP Competencies		Self-assessment	Solutions
	-Syntactic Competence: You can use a variety of sentence structures and a range of phonological features (stress, intonation patterns, pitch, and volume) to convey subtle shifts in purpose, meaning, and attitude. -Textual Competence: You can conform to stylistic conventions and requirements, based on communicative purposes and needs in academic fields and professional communication. Teamwork ability shown in academic communication; academic Self-concept demonstrated in academic communication.		
Academic value judgement and dissemination abilities	You can judge if the research publications in any formats have the right academic value focus. You are willing to take the responsibility and have the abilities to disseminate the research findings and academic values of Chinese researchers.		

2.1.2 Understanding Specific Academic English Communication Language Abilities Scales

The specific scales for both listening comprehension ability and oral expression academic abilities cover the following six aspects regardless of the speed and even the accents: oral description and understanding oral description, oral exposition and understanding oral exposition, oral instruction and understanding oral instruction, oral argumentation and understanding oral argumentation, oral interaction and understanding verbal interaction, and academic organizational competence.

UNIT 2 Cultivating Academic English Competencies

1) Oral Description and Understanding Oral Description

- Can understand oral descriptions of experiments in complex reports and extract key points and details.

2) Oral Exposition and Understanding Oral Exposition

- Can understand introductory descriptions of academic frontiers regardless of speech rate and comprehend the latest development in the field.
- Can present one's own research in detail and respond to questions coherently and logically at international conferences in his/her field.
- Can elaborate on abstract and complex issues, such as national policy, principles, and systems.
- Can give a detailed explanation and interpretation of articles or speeches with relatively abstract content.
- Can offer a lucid explanation of abstract theories.
- Can accurately convey the main ideas and supporting details in an academic lecture.
- Can give a detailed and coherent report of the research that he/she is undertaking, such as reporting a project's progress or current priorities.
- Can interpret or explain complex issues using logical analysis, such as identifying priorities and highlighting essential points.
- Can give a detailed explanation of topics in one's own field in a logical and comprehensible manner.
- Can give a coherent oral report of the procedure and result of an experiment or investigation.

3) Oral Instruction and Understanding Oral Instruction

- Can extract key points and procedures from multi-step/complex technical operation instructions regardless of speech rate and accent.
- Can understand procedures for experiments in one's own field regardless of speech rate.

4) Oral Argumentation and Understanding Oral Argumentation

- Can understand academic lectures containing technical terms related to one's own field and comprehend the main content.
- Can understand academic conference presentations or debates in one's own field and evaluate speakers' main points.

- Can understand academic discussions or talks in one's own field and extract key concepts and main ideas.

5) Oral Interaction and Understanding Verbal Interaction

- Can understand conversations containing low-frequency colloquial expressions or jargon regardless of speech rate; and extract main ideas and supporting details.
- Can evaluate the rationality and logic of opinions of different sides when participating in impassioned academic discussions.
- Can understand group interviews regardless of speech rate and accent and identify the opinions of the interviewees.

6) Academic Organizational Competence (Grammatical Competence, Vocabulary Competence, Syntactic Competence and Textual Competence)

- Can accurately-naturally use the grammatical and discourse knowledge in English oral communication; organize (choose, analyze, summarize, and synthesize) a variety of information to construct coherent and logical texts in academic or professional settings; apply (common) academic and professional vocabulary, a variety of sentence structures and a range of phonological features (stress, intonation patterns, pitch, and volume) to convey subtle shifts in purpose, meaning, and attitude, conforming to stylistic conventions and requirements, based on communicative purposes and needs in academic fields and professional communication.
- Can understand and use appropriately in listening and speaking the complex profession-specific grammatical forms, including nominalization in the contexts of science and technology, for example, "Electronic computers are applied to..." can be rewritten as "The applications of electronic computers...", which is a nominalization of the former.

› Tasks

❶ Summarize the ability objectives and fill in the following form.

	Abilities	Ability objectives
1	Description	
2	Exposition	
3	Instruction	

UNIT 2 Cultivating Academic English Competencies

(cont.)

	Abilities	Ability objectives
4	Argumentation	
5	Interaction	
6	Organization	

❷ **What research methods are mentioned in the following abstract? Read more abstracts of the articles in your field, identify the research methods and try to introduce them to your class.**

Academic Self-concept and the English Competencies Among English Learners in the University of the Immaculate Conception

English is the dominant international language in communications, science, aviation, entertainment, radio and diplomacy. The global spread of English becomes a serious economic and political disadvantage to those who do not possess a reasonable command of the language since English remains the primary language used in schools and universities and the majority of educational materials and references are printed in English. Learning to use English is of great importance today because academic communication tasks relate primarily in the use of English in international context. The purpose of this study was to investigate the relationship between the academic self-concept and the competencies in English among English learners in the University of Immaculate Conception. This study made the use of the descriptive correlation method to determine the relationship of academic self-concept and the English competencies among the English learners in UIC. Stratified random sampling was used to determine the appropriate sample size per program. Based on the results of this study, self-confidence in academics as one of the indicators of the academic self-concept has a significant relationship with one of the competencies in English among the respondents. Thus, the teachers should be offered methodological guidance in order to work on this psycho-educational intervention that may serve as an avenue to improve academic performance.

Keywords: Self-concept, English competencies, descriptive correlation, stratified random sampling

❸ **You are expected to work on one kind of ability in the ability list of Task 1. Consider your academic topic and research focus, and then decide what activity you will do to practise the target ability, what your academic topic is and what problem you may have by following the 4 steps of starting an academic activity.**

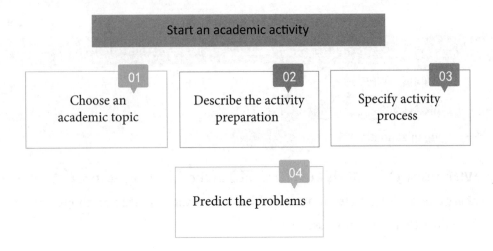

2.1.3 Locating the Gap Between Your Language Abilities and the Standards

To aim at the academic pragmatic goal of communicating smoothly using a style of language with remarkable effectiveness to achieve a desired outcome, students are suggested to know where they are by checking those ability requirements in Section 2.1.2 one by one.

Researchers on academic English competencies have proposed, for example, a four-facet connotation framework enlightened by a global survey of twenty universities, including more than language abilities, academic cognitive abilities, cross-cultural academic pragmatic communication abilities and learning abilities.

The article (in Task 2 of Section 2.1.2) can also guide students to have a clearer concept of their academic English abilities.

> Tasks

❶ **Put your strengths and weaknesses down and summarize them orally after reckoning the gap between your own and the required academic communication abilities.**

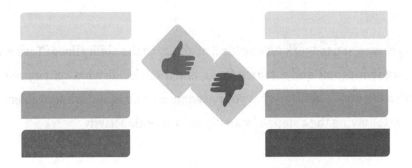

UNIT 2 Cultivating Academic English Competencies

❷ A group critical assessment on the summary done in Task 1 will be advised and each group representative will be invited to deliver a brief group report of the assessment.

❸ Describe one of these academic activities you have participated in and analyze the language problems you failed in dealing with.

Problem 1: _____
Problem 2: _____
Cause analysis: _____

〉Language Toolkit

Useful Sentence Patterns of Diagnosing and Surveying Academic English Language Competencies:

- I have some difficulties in…
- When doing…, it's hard for me to…
- During the process of…, it's probably that we meet some difficulties. For example, …
- Though I have done…, I still can't…
- This survey on…is designed to…
- It can be seen in the survey that…
- Among the several aspects of…, what is most difficult for me is…
- In addition to…, there are also other factors pertaining to…
- It is obviously concluded from the survey that…
- The survey result describes/predicts/reveals…
- As for the difference between…, I will summarize as follows…
- Considering…, I hold that…
- There are…steps to do…, of which I will introduce…
- Despite…, there are some opportunities to…if we make efforts to…
- What should arouse our attention is that…
- Compared to discussion, presentation requires…
- There were some problems when I did…

- I found it almost impossible to...
- It is so obvious that I have some demerits in...

> **Reflection & Practice**

1. What are other possible factors rather than English language abilities that may hinder you from effective academic English oral communication?
2. Think about all those ineffective cases in your academic communication and point out the reason.
3. Check the academic English communication language ability list one by one to see what is the hardest for you. Write them down and present your report to the class.
4. Discuss with your team and the whole class about how to practise value judgement and take academic responsibilities as a beginner researcher.

2.2 Ways to Improve Academic Communication Competencies

Classroom Voice

With a good understanding of the competencies and the academic scenarios, Anna thinks it is time to take measures to improve her communication ability in practice. But what are the effective ways to perform better in the academic English Communication?

Instructor's Voice

Do you know any ways to improve your academic English communication ability? Work in groups to discuss about the satisfactory measures you have gained. Make sense of the important concepts of how to cultivate academic communication abilities and get ready to learn more effective strategies.

2.2.1 Improving Academic Communication Language Abilities

Academic communication abilities are the synthesis of language ability, positive self-concept, teamwork ability, critical thinking, and cross-culture ability. Most English communication usually requires all of your integrate performance. It's time to reckon on what countermeasures can be taken to improve your academic English oral communication and listening competencies. Academic communication English is open for participants to use English in a general academic context of globalization and internationalization. "Academic communication English practitioners need to engage in or with research into the dominant discourse norms in academia and raise awareness of these norms while encouraging the application of norms in a context-sensitive way." (Blaj-Ward, 2017: 59)

Given the variations among academic contexts, students need to work as active learners, partners or researchers in the real academic contexts to exploit the interdependent abilities between linguistic abilities of standardization, accuracy, completeness, logical sequence and conciseness of academic expression and the non-linguistic abilities such as critical thinking, professional knowledge and academic cross-cultural communication.

1) Organizing an Oral Exposition

Though in both academic conversations and monologues, speakers may narrate the development of a research topic/theory/method, tell a story of his own academic experience, survey the telling of a research story, especially in field research, describe experiments in the academic reports by extracting key points and details, and so on. Academic oral communication mostly adopts expository method in reports and presentations, argumentative method in discussion and debate, and interaction and organization in all of those scenarios.

Oral exposition is a type of oral discourse used to explain, describe, give information or inform. The creator of an expository text can't assume that the listener has prior knowledge or prior understanding of the topic being discussed.

One important point to keep in mind for the speaker is to try to use words that clearly show what they are talking about rather than blatantly telling what is being discussed. Since clarity requires strong organization, one of the most important mechanisms that can be used to improve our skills in exposition is to provide directions to improve the organization of the content.

2) Shaping Oral Expository Organizational Patterns

Oral academic exposition has its organizational patterns of circumlocution, narrative interspersion, recursion, description, sequences, comparison, cause-effect, and problem-solution.

We can put a multiple facet outline for an expository task. For example:

Contexts: present a research program/update a progress/respond to a submission;

Audiences/Listeners: peers/supervisors/editors;

Purposes: inform/persuade;

Aids: PowerPoint slides/videos/printed materials.

3) Making an Oral Argument

Although an argument deals with opinions, objectivity and reliability rather than subjectivity must be conformed to in an academic oral argument. There are two main methods of argumentation in academic contexts—inductive method and deductive method.

Inductive method is a way of reasoning from particular facts to general conclusions. It is a process of discovering and testing the hypotheses by collecting the evidence, making a hypothesis to explain the evidence and investigating to see whether the hypothesis fits the evidence, which is commonly used as a scientific method.

Deductive method is reasoning from general to specific, from the general principle (the major premise), to its application to the fact (the minor premise), then to a conclusion.

4) Cultivating Oral Organizational Competence

You should check the following aspects:

Grammatical knowledge: e.g. nominalization;

Discourse knowledge: e.g. constructing coherent and logical texts;

(Common) academic and professional vocabulary: referring to the word list;

Sentence structures: e.g. complex sentences, inversion, parallel structures;

Phonological features: e.g. stress, intonation patterns, pitch, and volume;

Stylistic conventions and requirements: e.g. logical, accessible and retrievable.

5) Four Practical Strategies

Identification and extraction: When preparing and delivering an oral academic discourse, you need to make sure for your audience, the topic, the purpose, the main structure/ the hierarchy, the main details and so on, are clearly stated so that they can be identified easily by your audience. Meanwhile, in order to follow the speaker and understand an oral academic context well, you need to do as your audience can do to make full use of the structural and topical clues when attending a lecture, a seminar or a discussion.

Summarization and analysis: Academic speakers will have to summarize and analyze what they have collected for an academic communication purpose. They may summarize and analyze the historical documents, the published papers or their own research findings and conclusions. In the process of analyzing and summarizing, experienced academic speakers usually focus on the development clues, the main points and especially the relation among them, putting them in a table or in a mind map.

As an academic reader or listener, you are strongly suggested to take notes of a speech in the same way how a writer or a speaker has prepared it. After analyzing the identified topic, the hierarchy, the main details, and the main transitional conjunctions, you can get a summary.

UNIT 2 Cultivating Academic English Competencies

> Tasks

❶ Listen to an academic speech from some public academic speech resources. Identify and discuss with your group members about its manifestation of academic discourse features.

1. Phonological features (e.g. sentence stress; intonation patterns):

   _____

2. Vocabulary features (e.g. conciseness; preciseness):

   _____

3. Sentence structures (e.g. simple sentences; complex sentences):

   _____

4. Discourse features (e.g. signal words; cohesive devices):

   _____

5. Grammatical features (e.g. nominalization; tense/aspect distribution):

   _____

6. Stylistic features (e.g. expository; persuasive):

   _____

❷ Apply the expository skills to introduce one research term, or the development of a theory or a method in your field, and assess your talk from the five aspects.

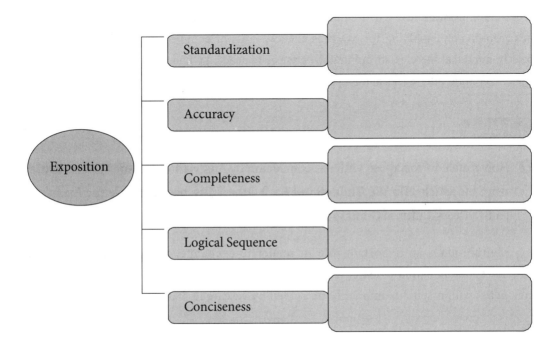

2.2.2 Enhancing Academic English Non-language Abilities

1) Academic Self-concept in Academic Communication

To build a positive academic self-concept, you'd better take an active attitude towards academic communication by making full preparation such as reading more about the topic of the lecture, reading regularly top English journals in your field to keep yourself informed of the latest research findings, if you have not made any achievements currently like a published paper or a desirable English language self-efficacy.

2) Teamwork Ability Shown in Academic Communication

With postgraduate or above education or a competent academic practitioner, teamworking is an important ability to ensure a good academic performance, establish a more cooperative academic personality and pave a more smooth way to academic success.

3) Critical Thinking in Academic Communication

Critical thinking is a way of logical thinking, an attitude toward academic acquisition and a habit prompted in whatever academic context. Innovation will be impossible without critical thinking. Critical thinking is required throughout each step of academic communication. To develop advanced critical thinking ability, students are encouraged and supposed to improve the ability of disagreeing with the existing research results, illustrating their own views or creating a new idea based on the previous studies.

4) Cross-cultural Abilities in International Academic Communication

There is no national boundaries in terms of academic communication. Establish a strong cross-cultural awareness when communicating with international researchers and experts, or consulting and applying for overseas studies, visits or conferences and so forth. Always bear in mind that there exists cultural differences in academic communication. Beware of the specific cultural differences and prepare yourself well with the knowledge.

> Tasks

❶ **How much do you agree with the conclusion by Austrian Professor Markus Kittler from his article "Do We Understand Each Other? Discussing Academic Exchange from a Cross-Cultural Communication Perspective"?**

Culture plays an important role in academic exchange, and insights from cross-cultural communication research can help to enhance communication quality. Research conducted within settings implicitly perceived by researchers as mono-cultural regarding country, industry, or organization (e.g., a phenomenon studied within an organization in the researcher's home country) still does contain cross-cultural elements as it usually involves members from two (different) cultures: academics and practitioners. This observation lends additional importance to the often-neglected role of the cross-cultural lens and adds to the relevance of our model for business and management research.

❷ How to be a good team member and how to think critically ? Discuss with your group members. And write down your summary and report it to the class.

Tips: _____

_____

_____

Summary: _____

_____

_____

_____

2.2.3 Grasping Essential Skills for Communication in the Main Oral Academic Scenarios

Oral academic communication may involve making or attending a dialogue or a monologue. A monologue can be a speech, a lecture, a presentation, etc. whilst dialogue can be a panel discussion, questions & answers, etc. They are mostly on:

- literature retrieval/management/annotation/review;
- research methodology (quantitative research vs qualitative research, specific research methods, including survey, questionnaires, case study, experiment, simulation, measurement, modeling, data analysis, content analysis, and field study, etc.);
- research theories (general research theories vs specific research theories);
- personal academic development (academic interest, academic direction, thesis defense, essay/paper submission, project application and implement, etc.);
- academic activities (seminar, workshop, lecture, international academic conference, etc.).

Among the various academic scenarios above, academic speakers, such as students or researchers, more often show up or are involved in the following four aspects, and usually adopt these five competences together with the pragmatic strategies to achieve their communicative goals.

1) Attending a Lecture or a Report

If you find it hard to listen to a professor or a specialized researcher, you are not alone. However, compared with other discourses, academic lectures are more topic-centered and well-developed on a given academic topic. The theme, key points and main examples from a lecture are unfolded clearly and usually in emphatic tones. Generalized sentences and transitional expressions are often used for listeners to follow the lecturer more easily. Identifying the important information of a lecture requires active listening and taking notes well.

For preparation, a paper handout or a digital version of the brief introduction to the subject and the speaker is always offered to the attendees beforehand, with the help of which you are suggested to obtain more knowledge about the topic of the lecture and its speaker's academic achievements on this topic. Also, if you can stay awake and be an active listener during the lecture, through being ready to predict, concentrating on the lecture, and taking down the notes of the main information in a four-level structural mind map, you will have a good understanding of the lecture.

2) Making a Report or a Presentation

Students are to report with or without visual aids like slides, their selection of a research topic, the summary and reviews of their reading of the academic list, the periodical progress of the experiment, and so on regularly; or they may be invited to present their research paper at an academic conference.

Think about the question: How and in what order will you make a report to audience? With a clear and specific answer to this question, you can start with an outline of the structure of your report or presentation. You will not fail if you can also be confident enough to present fluently what you will have prepared and remember to communicate, with appropriate tones and body language, when necessary.

3) Participating in a Discussion

There are a lot of opportunities for students to discuss with their peers or with their supervisors in the class, the research group or in a seminar or a workshop.

Preparation is possible and necessary if it is not an impromptu discussion. You may take time to write down the core of your stand and your idea, collect convincing evidence to support you in the discussion. Then you get ready to join in a discussion, seize the key points of the speaker's idea and express your own neatly.

You may support or oppose partly or totally the main idea, the development of the idea or the supporting details from other participants in the discussion. Therefore, appropriate expressions and right strategies should be taken for the right contexts. Whatever the context is, you're always suggested to talk even argue in a powerful but polite manner.

4) Sitting in an Interview

Being in an interview for an academic post or for further academic study, your academic background and achievements are expected in your self-introduction. You'd better prepare a written CV so that you only need to make a slight alteration to meet a specific interview goal. Being confident, polite and modest, but active in responding to the questions will leave a good impression on the interviewers.

〉Tasks

❶ Compare the major differences between academic English monologues and dialogues.

	Monologue (Presentation/Speech)	Academic dialogue
Number of speaker(s)		
Audience		
Visual aids		
Topics		
Formality		

❷ Check if you are familiar with the major scenarios in Section 2.2.3, discuss with your group what abilities are expected in these main scenarios, and write them down.

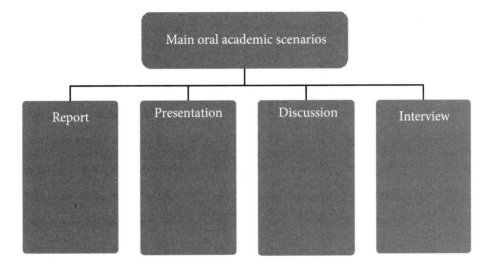

Language Toolkit

Useful Sentence Patterns of Enhancing Academic English Competencies:

- There are difficulties ahead though, I will make efforts to...
- Practice makes perfect. Taking effective measures counts for more.
- It is fundamental for researchers to be professionally knowledgeable since...
- Among the research theories/methods, ...will be introduced in...aspects.
- When it comes to team work and critical thinking, we should bear in mind that...
- Whether an academic concept is positive or not, it's up to...
- The more..., the more confident and the more opportunities we will...

Reflection & Practice

1. In what way do you think academic English competencies will bring more international academic opportunities and confidence?
2. Why will a good command of academic knowledge enhance a positive self-concept?
3. Make a presentation on the self diagnosis of your strengths and weaknesses of academic English. Try to conform to the academic English competency requirements and follow the instructor's voice.
4. Read the following article for further discussion:

Science as a career attracts people from across the world. But whether researchers come from Beijing, Berlin or Buenos Aires, they have to express most of their ideas and findings in English. Having a dominant language can streamline the process of science, but it also creates extra barriers and the potential for conflict.

Researchers who are not fluent in English often face hurdles beyond learning a new language. Nature asked seven researchers Source: with personal or professional experience of language barriers to share their insights.

(Source: Woolston, C. & Osório, J. 2019. When English is not your mother tongue. 06–10. From *Nature* website.)

Part Two

Stepping into Academia

Unit 3
Accessing Academic English Literature

Learning Objectives

- To get a better understanding of genres, formats and distribution of literature;

- To grasp the basic academic literature retrieval and collection methods and common retrieval software;

- To briefly report the procedures of retrieving academic English literature;

- To understand the value norms of academic literature.

Pre-learning Questions

1. How much do you know about the classification of literature databases?
2. How do you usually search for your literature?
3. What are the major problems you have encountered so far in accessing academic English literature?
4. How do you distinguish high quality literature from low quality literature?

It is never too emphatic to lay the greatest emphasis on literature for scholars to start their academic research when they all agree that no research can be done without any basis or referring to the previous studies. Literature, therefore, becomes one of the first tasks research beginners are expected to have access to. Its genres and formats, classification, retrieving and screening, tracking and retrieving software are among the basic academic knowledge that will prepare you to step into the academia. In addition, we're going to find out the distribution structure of academic literature achievements in the current world, the representative research literature by the Chinese academia in your subject area and the way they related to the global research development and its tendency. What is the accumulation and flow of academic achievements in the process of academic exchanges between China and other countries?

3.1 Literature Sources and Types

Classroom Voice

Jenny is often told by her supervisors and the academic peers that literature plays a crucial role in research since it is mostly the source of the historical and current published research results. Papers are the only form of literature she knows when it comes to the question what literature is.

Instructor's Voice

Although students from different majors do various research programs, it's better for you to have a good knowledge of effective literature accesses and academic English literature ranging from types, formats to features, which will ensure you a smooth start of your academic journey so that you will not be faced with the problems Jenny has with literature.

3.1.1 Literature Sources

Academic English literature can be divided into three general types according to how original they are.

Table 3.1 Three General Types of Academic English Literature

Primary (Original source material)	**Secondary** (Source that analyzes, evaluates, and interprets primary source material)	**Tertiary** (Summaries or condensed versions of primary and secondary source material)
Archival material	Biography	Abstracts
Artifacts	Books	Bibliography
Autobiographies (books)	Book reviews	Chronology
Correspondence	Conference proceedings	Dictionary
Diaries	Dissertation	Directories
Government documents	Editorial	Encyclopedias
Interview	Literary criticism	Guidebooks
Letters	Magazines articles	Manuals
Journals	Textbooks	Indexes
Manuscript	Treatise	
Memoirs (books)	Scholarly journal articles	
Newspapers		
Photographs		
Works of art (music, painting, poetry, etc.)		

1) Primary Sources

The interpretation of primary source is dependent upon the field of study. However, the most common definition pertains to the originality of the material. It is an original or seminal source, artifact, or evidence that has not been changed in any shape or form. These sources offer a first-hand account of an experiment, event, and/or experience related to a particular moment in time. Original documents include speeches, diaries, manuscripts, interviews, letters, official records, taped recordings, original news footage, and researcher's video documentation. Autobiographies and memoirs are also considered primary resources although the content material is documented after the original events took place.

Empirical research is one of the main sources learners and scholars will use to support their work. Its data is gathered through observation, experimentation, and testing. It is vital to a doctoral learner's development to frequently read and use this type of primary source. Empirical research is normally published in journal articles and/or periodicals, but other types of research can be found, such as reviews and reports. Journal articles can occupy both primary and secondary source identification depending on the discipline and source of knowledge. Primary sources are cited and referred to by secondary sources for a variety of reasons and motivations, but mainly to support, criticize, comment, investigate, build, and/or expand on a subject.

2) Secondary Sources

A secondary source refers to written or recorded material that interprets, analyzes, or evaluates primary sources in a way that suggests the written narrative is one or more steps removed from the original material. Some examples include journal articles, research studies, essays, reviews, presentations, magazine articles, books, textbooks, and book reviews. Ideally, doctoral learners will have access to primary resources, but depending on the study's focus and methodology, secondary sources can play a dominant role in learners' understanding of their field, especially when it comes to constructing a comprehensive literature review section for a prospectus, and, eventually, a dissertation.

3) Tertiary Sources

These sources generally are summaries or condensed versions of primary and secondary sources. Often, these sources are related to reference materials, such as dictionaries, encyclopedias, reference guides, and indexes.

› Tasks

❶ Categorize the sources you often use into the three groups.

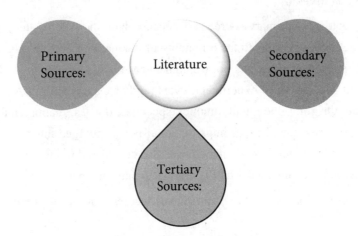

UNIT 3 Accessing Academic English Literature

❷ What research are the literature sources respectively fit for? Offer your reasons.

Literature sources	Research types/purposes	Reasons
Primary		
Secondary		
Tertiary		

3.1.2 Major Literature Types

Besides in-text citation, references at the end of the paper are indicated by their initial letters according to the cited literature types. The following are the major literature types and their respective initial letters:

Monograph [M]

Conference [C]

Journal [J]

Dissertation [D]

Newspaper [N]

Report [R]

Standard [S]

Patent [P]

Database [DB]

Computer Program [CP]

Electronic Bulletin Board [EB]

Archive [A]

Cartographic Material [CM]

Dataset [DS]

Others [Z]

1) Academic Journals

Among the literature types, academic journals and papers attract most attention of researchers.

Academic journals are peer-reviewed periodicals issued by an institution, corporation or a professional or a scholarly society in which researchers publish current news or reports in the form of articles of their research work.

Students are suggested to find out the top academic journals in their fields and keep tracking them for all the major most current research findings, or specifically on a research topic you take your academic interest in.

2) Types of Papers

Academic papers are usually peer-reviewed papers, including original articles, letters/brief reports, review articles, editorials, correspondence or communication, whose titles are a narration or a question, whose abstracts are descriptive, informative, informative-descriptive, and so on, and which usually apply an aim/problem–method–results–conclusion format.

Tasks

❶ Write down the full names of the following reference abbreviations.

[M] [C] [J] [D] [N] [R] [S] [P] [DB] [CP] [EB] [A] [CM] [DS] [Z]

_____

_____

_____

❷ Introduce one of the peer-reviewed academic journals in your field, its structure and the reference requirements.

Name of the journal: _____

Its structure: _____

Reference requirements: _____

Language Toolkit

Useful Sentence Patterns of Talking About Academic English Literature Reference Requirements:

- As for English literature, no researchers can proceed without...
- It's not tough to identify...if we read/observe...
- ...among various literature genres, peer-reviewed papers/articles are...
- Although most articles share a similar structure, there are...

- Among the top academic journals in my field, my regular focus is on...
- There are some requirements by this journal as follows...
- ...represents..., which means/covers...

> Reflection & Practice

1. Which type of literature source do researchers in your field usually use? Reckon on the reasons.
2. What academic journals do you regularly read and track? Check, list and report their features to the class.
3. Exemplify those required literature for your researches referring to the introduction of academic sources and identify their literature genres, formats and functions of the attributes.

3.2 Retrieval Databases, Methods and Strategies

Classroom Voice

Richard finds it hard and frustrating to know how to search for the literature efficiently when he wants to write an introduction to or a review of the previous studies. Or there might be a too long list of retrieval results or no relevant literature can be found at all, which slow his pace of work. Thus he wants to grasp more effective research tools and methods.

Instructor's Voice

A handy tool makes a handy man. Researchers surely need to know how to obtain the required literature they expect especially with a clear mind of what their research theme is and what the documents types are. Each is suggested to lay his focus on those retrieval tools and databases that are helpful in their studies and researches. Try to set your search goal and retrieve academic documents, find out your difficulties in retrieving documents.

3.2.1 Retrieval Databases

It is of great significance to retrieve literature since it is a time-saving and effective way to obtain academic and professional knowledge, keep researchers updated with research findings so as to determine research topics, increase their accurate judgement and acceptance of new frontier knowledge if they have a good mastery of retrieval resources. Here are some retrieval databases recommended in Table 3.2.

Table 3.2 Some Retrieval Databases Recommended

Comprehensive retrieval databases	Websites
SCI (Science Citation Index)	https://www.sci.com
SSCI (Social Sciences Citation Index)	https://www.ssci.com
Engineering Village (EI: The Engineering Index)	https://www.engineeringvillage.com
IEEE	https://ieeexplore.ieee.org
Google Scholar	https://scholar.glgoo.org/
SCI-HUB	https://sci-hub.tw/
Web of Science	http://app.webofknowledge.com/
Wanfang	https://www.wanfangdata.com.cn/index.html
CiteSeerx	https://citeseerx.ist.psu.edu/
High Wire	https://highwire.stanford.edu//
Ebsco	https://www.ebscohost.com
Proquest	https://www.proquest.com
Wiley Online Library	https://oninelibrary.wiley.com
Elsevier	https://www.elsevier.com
ChaoXing	http://ss.chaoxing.com

Each database has its own features, therefore researchers had better know what they are. Here are some examples.

1) Scopus

As the largest abstract and citation database of peer-reviewed literature, Scopus delivers an overview of the world's research output in the fields of science, technology, medicine, social sciences and arts and humanities. Content from over 5,000 publishers is easily tracked, analyzed and visualized.

2) ScienceDirect

This is Elsevier's leading information solution that empowers over 15 million researchers, teachers, students, health care professionals and information professionals around the world to ensure that their work has more impact. Science Direct combines authoritative, full-text scientific, technical and health publications with smart, intuitive functionality so users can stay more informed and can work more effectively and efficiently. With over 14 million publications from over 3,800 journals and more than 35,000 books from Elsevier, their imprints and their society partners, Science Direct empowers smarter research.

3) Springerlink

Springerlink provides researchers with access to millions of scientific, technical and medical documents (STM) from journals, books, series, protocols, reference works and proceedings. It has alerts and favorites services, and its online first TM can track literature.

4) Ebsco

Ebsco has over 100 online literature databases, two of which are Academic Search Premier and Business Source Premier.

› Tasks

❶ **Check the above databases to see if you have access to them, and recommend two or three that are most often used in your research field and briefly introduce their merits.**

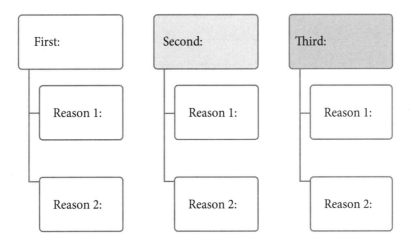

❷ **Make a list and introduce the specialized databases of your research field.**

My research field: _____

Specialized databases: _____

Features: _____

3.2.2 Search Terms for Retrieval

Though retrieval databases have their own featured services, they have most search terms in common. If you are familiar with these, your search will speed up. The following words are often found in the searching webpage and can navigate you to achieve diverse search objectives:

author, affiliation, annual, archive, article, authorize, available, access, accessibility, abstract, bibliographic, brief, browse, citation, chronological, clear, collection, copyright, category, discipline, default, dissertation, documentation, database, easy search, advanced search, export, extract, ESI (Essential Science Indicators), FAQ, field, full-text, keywords, hypertext database, ISBN, ISSN, issue, index, IF (impact factor), journal, keywords, navigation, newsletter, peer-reviewed, publish, range, reset, review, remote access, sort, submit, subscribe, times cited, related records, update, volume.

> **Tasks**

❶ **Read and explain the following search terms to your classmate orally.**

Archive: _____

Affiliation: _____

Chronological: _____

Hypertext databases: _____

ISBN: _____

ISSN: _____

Peer-reviewed: _____

Impact factor: _____

❷ Report to the class the given information of the upcoming conferences in Figure 3.1 and demonstrate the searching function of some special terms in Figure 3.2.

Figure 3.1   A Screenshot of IEEE Webpage

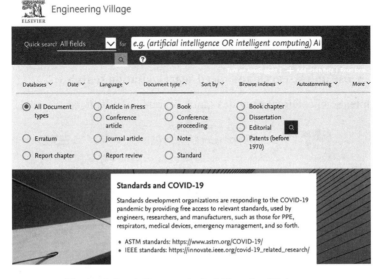

Figure 3.2   A Screenshot of Elsevier Webpage

3.2.3 Retrieving Methods

1) Classification of Retrieving Methods

There are several methods of searching academic documents, including direct method, check method and sample method and so forth.

- **Direct method:** Direct method is retrieving bibliographic and chronological information in the order of time to collect systematic literature about a larger subject.

- **Check method:** The emphasis of check method lies in recent literature, by which the latest literature can be obtained as quickly as possible. It is mostly used for newly opened topics or old topics with new content. What is needed is recently published documents in order to grasp the level of the topic in the recent period.

- **Sample method:** The premise of using the time-saving sample method requires that the researchers should be very familiar with the characteristics of subject development, otherwise it is difficult to achieve the expected results.

- **Retrospective method:** The advantage of the retrospective method is that it is intuitive, convenient, and you can trace a large number of references on a particular topic. This is a good way to expand the source of information without or with incomplete retrieval tools.

Retrieving the literature obtaining a more systematic literature clue from the perspective of the disciplinary system, that is, it has a tribal retrieval function. The content features, external characteristic approaches and professional indexes work jointly for a search goal. When necessary, a comprehensive retrieval method may ensure precision and save labor.

2) Steps of Retrieving Literature Online

Step 1: Identify your purpose of retrieval

Step 2: Select a retrieval tool/a database/an index

Step 3: Choose quick search/advanced search/citation search

For example, ScienceDirect provides quick search and advanced search as in Figure 3.3.

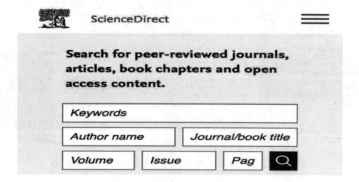

Figure 3.3 Quick Search of ScienceDirect

The above Figure 3.3 is quick search. Researchers can enter their search terms in the boxes of keywords, author name, journal title, volume, issue, page, and so on.

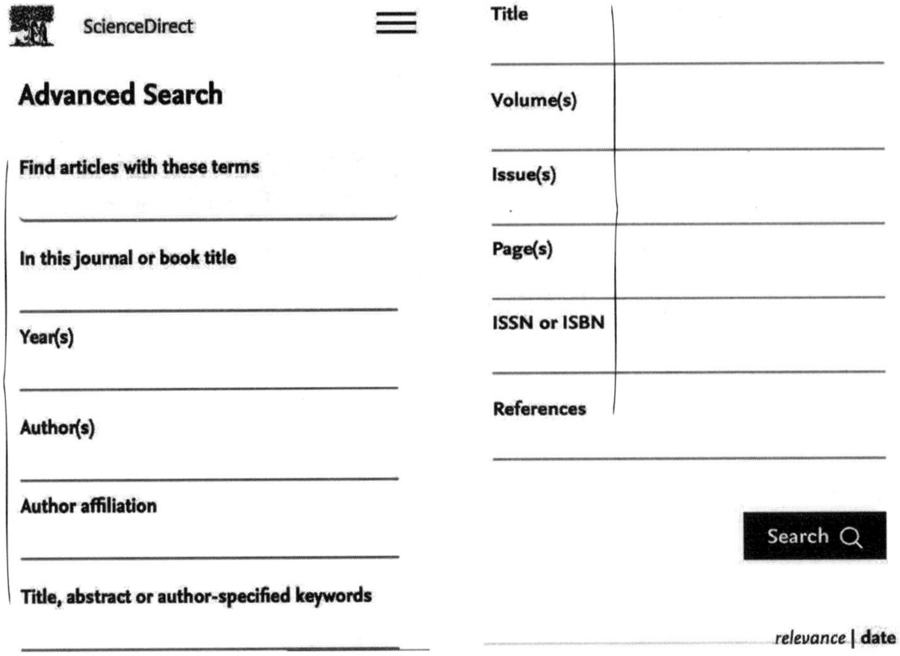

Figure 3.4 Advanced Search

Researchers can also use advanced search as shown in Figure 3.4, with more details about the literature, like author affiliation, title, abstract or author-specified keywords, volumes, issues, ISSN, references and so on. Results can show in relevance or by date.

Wiley Online Library has Citation Search service. It allows searchers to input the items for the name of a journal from the given list in alphabetic order, then year, volume, issue, page, and citation# (number).

Step 4: Start to use the Boolean Operators

These operators must be entered in UPPERCASE to work. Question mark (?) is used to replace in a search term to represent a single character (e.g. wom?n finds women or woman). Refine or adjust the search elements when necessary.

Defining the keywords in retrieving is one of the toughest parts. Synonyms of the keywords and the recommended or relevant keywords provided on the searching page will usually offer a new opportunity when the results fail the searching purpose with your selected keywords. CNKI index, Nano, and proposal analysis of Baidu Scholar serve the similar purpose.

Step 5: Select the list of the search results

Research results are mostly selected or rearranged in time sequence or by relevance to meet the retrieval purpose (as shown in Figure 3.5).

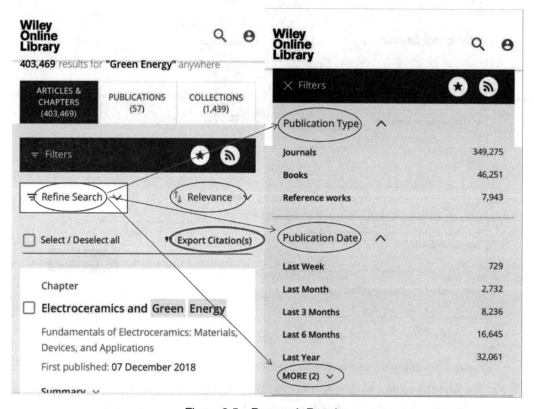

Figure 3.5　Research Results

Step 6: Filter and refine the research results

Also, if the search results are not satisfying, filter the research results and refine the research fields and the chosen retrieval elements like the publication date, the publication type, the domain, and others. Read those with no accessibility, and save, download or export the citation or those with accessibility into the document management tool for further reading.

UNIT 3 Accessing Academic English Literature

> **Tasks**

❶ Describe the steps of your retrieving for a research topic.

Your research topic:

Steps:

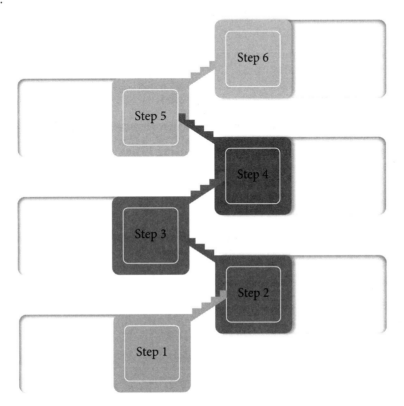

❷ Make an oral report of both the findings and the problems in each step with the help of the following table.

	Step 1	Step 2	Step 3	Step 4	Step 5	Step 6
Findings						
Problems						

3.2.4 Retrieving Strategies

The retrieval strategy is an information retrieval scheme designed for retrieval questions and the use of retrieval access and technology. The purpose is to achieve a certain precision and efficiency. Analyze issues and develop search strategies, find literature with search tools and then request original documents based on the source.

Students are afterwards to present their search goal(s), how they refine their retrieval formula, what the search domain(s) are and briefly report their individual searching process together with their findings in their academic community. They are also anticipated to offer suggestions for better and more efficient research results.

The merits and demerits of using these retrieval tools and data bases will be collected, thus a group/class survey on retrieving academic literature will be taken for a further discussion. Students from similar academic backgrounds will be suggested to work in the same group.

Step 1: Set a specific and precise research goal

Step 2: Define the keywords, and restrict related elements pertained to the search scope

Step 3: Compare the searching results by using two or more databases

› Tasks

❶ Present your retrieval practice procedures of searching for the literature by adopting the following three steps and tips.

Search goals: _____

Search scope/databases: _____

Search domains/the publication/the date: _____

Search retrieval formula: _____

_____

Search results: _____

❷ Discuss with your group members on how much your search results satisfy your search goals. A check list is suggested.

My Search Goals	vs	My Search Results

UNIT 3 Accessing Academic English Literature

> **Language Toolkit**

Useful Sentence Patterns of Discussing Accessing Academic English Literature:

- It's beneficial for a researcher to be kept updated with...
- To meet the purpose of my research, I collect the historical literature on the development of...
- The features of this retrieving tool are...
- This database...is better than the similar ones in that...
- In order to..., it is highly suggested that...
- To start with, ...What's more...
- Retrieving academic English documents involves these steps...
- I find it hard to identify my search goal when I have a vague topic for the new research.

> **Reflection & Practice**

1. What methods are more suitable to search for the relevant literature for your current research?
2. What makes your retrieval hard to achieve your search goal?
3. Prepare a report on your overall academic direction or one aspect of your academic direction, based on the literature you will retrieve by adopting two or more of the retrieval methods.
4. Work with the classmates from your direction/field to find out the distribution of the research literature in your direction/field and describe the development of the literature. How many are done by Chinese writers? What can you see from the distribution map and the development trajectory?

3.3 Tracking and Ordering Literature

Classroom Voice

To keep updated with the latest literature, Alice is offered the email or message reminder service by many databases and retrieval software of tracking and ordering the literature she needs most immediately after they are officially published. It is amazing to see the updates for her when she opens her email box.

Instructor's Voice

Alice, like many graduate student, is wondering how she can keep herself updated with the latest literature in her research field, thus she will be able to accomplish her assignments in team discussion and ensure she will not miss any latest references in her paper writing.

3.3.1 Literature Tracking and Ordering Tools

References play different roles at the stages of research as shown in Figure 3.6. It's time-consuming to open each official website of the academic journals or do manual retrieving of the literature that has been most recently published. Some tracking and ordering tools are highly recommended and introduced.

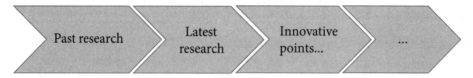

Figure 3.6 Different Stages of Research

1) Mendeley Suggest

Databases or retrieval tools like Mendeley mostly provide the suggestion service according to your retrieval history and habits.

2) The Old Reader

With such a widely-used and friendly website, you can order the best academic journals, add your favourite websites, organize your academic interests and read articles as they are published on it.

3) ResearchGate

Updates of the prestigious researchers and publications you may follow will be sent to your registration company/organization/university email immediately after they are published. New recommendations will be posted automatically, too.

4) Pubmed and Pubcrawler

To track and order publishes for a specific area like health science, you can turn to Pubmed to create alerts on it, log onto My Account, choose frequency of the alerts under Journal Alerts, then you will be sent the updates if you allow the push alerts. Pubcraler provides the free alerting service that scans daily updates to the Pubmed and GenBank Databases.

UNIT 3 Accessing Academic English Literature

> **Tasks**

1 Discuss with your group members about whom (the authors) and what (the publications/the research areas/topics, etc.) to be tracked and ordered for your research and in your field. Make a list.

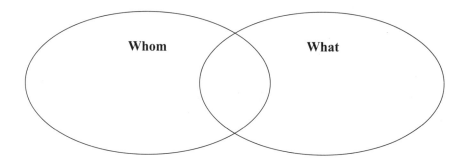

2 Try these recommended tracking and ordering tools. Record for at least one week what you track and order and what results you have on them.

Tools	Your ordering	Mon.	Tue.	Wed.	Thur.	Fri.	Sat.	Sun.
Mendeley Suggest								
The Old Reader								
ResearchGate								
Pubcrawler/ Pubmed								

3 Summarize your findings, and report your findings and problems that remain unsolved.

Findings: _____

_____

_____

Problems: _____

_____

_____

Solutions: _____

_____

_____

3.3.2 Challenges and Precautions

Though challenges might be there, here are some precautions for you to deal with them in retrieving academic literature.

- Follow the literature updates and take literature tracking as part of the regular academic life, which has been accepted as one of the most important academic competences. A fixed time every day or weekly will ensure you a good habit.
- It's not very hard to select your academic interest or your keywords for the newest publication alerts or suggestion. In addition, it usually takes much of your time since more than one thousand article are published there every day. It will be more frustrating and challenging in multiple or cross disciplinary fields. Identify what are the most related and hottest research topics via the latest contents of the most concerned journals.
- Alerts and suggestion are made referring to your search history and the articles you have searched or read. Too much reliance on it may prevent you from being exposed to some important research results. So following the top journals and authors can make it up.
- Give priority to the contents of the top journals and expand your search keywords, otherwise you will be very risky at missing the most important articles.
- Keep in touch with the frontier research results, cultivate your reading habit and take notes.
- Have a regular meeting or share with your workmates, friends or tutors.

❯ Tasks

❶ Describe your tracking habits and ordering preference.

_____

_____

_____

② **Practice these precautions in Section 3.3.2, share your achievements and also offer some other tips if you have.**

Your achievements and your tips:

_____

_____

_____

〉 Language Toolkit

Useful Sentence Patterns of Discussing Literature Searching Results:

- It's time-consuming to do manual tracking.
- It is really frustrating when emails show a great amount of unrelated articles.
- There remains a problem for me...
- I felt frustrated when I was told I had missed an important reference.
- Alerts are useless when the keywords are not specific enough.
- I'd like to share my experience of using tracking alerts.
- It's so exciting to gain literature competence of keeping updated with the newly-published articles and distinguishing between useful and useless ones.

〉 Reflection & Practice

1. Many famous experts hold that tracking the latest literature should become a daily or weekly regularity for researchers at all stages. Do you think the significance of literature tracking should be highlighted? Is it true that efficient tracking is part of academic competence?

2. Keep tracking for a specific research in this semester and report the references you have obtained.

3. Think about what makes academic articles or other research publication valuable. What are the possible norms or standards to judge their quality and value?

Unit 4
Managing Academic English Literature

Learning Objectives

- To learn to import, label, rank and annotate academic English literaturebased on the right academic judgement of the value of literature;

- To report how to use management tools in effective ways;

- To understand the important role of academic literature in optimizing knowledge structure, broadening academic vision and updating professional information;

- To evaluate the effectiveness of literature management.

Pre-learning Questions

1. What are your "standards" for selecting desired literature from the retrieval results?
2. Where do you usually import the academic English literature to?
3. What are the purposes of annotating English documents?

Feeling frustrated in managing academic literature seems a shared upsetting experience among researcher beginners when they lack the awareness of and skills in the mastery of academic literature management. Compared to the time-consuming word-file or PDF copy and save method, literature management tools like Endnote, Noteexpress, Mendeley, can improve the efficiency of sorting and collating the literature. To lay a solid foundation for literature management, researchers are required to understand the nature of literature and the value of literature, so that they know what literature will be selected and how it will be referred to in the researchers' own papers.

4.1 Reference Management Tools

Classroom Voice

Richard finds it so frustrating to have a long list of downloaded full-text papers. He used to store all the retrieved articles in a folder, though they are listed in editing time order or alphabetic order, he often realized that he couldn't find the article he wanted. More problems arose when he took notes of them and built links among them.

Instructor's Voice

What are your difficulties when you manage your imported literature? Recommend a management tool and use it to manage the literature for a current research. Take down the problems in the process and your smart way to manage them efficiently, and discuss with the group members.

4.1.1 Some English Literature Management Tools

Effective management of English literature is supportive of clearing the usual mess of the selected literature. When having a selected list from the retrieval results, you always harbour the hope that the accessible literature can be well-managed via the application of the most

UNIT 4　Managing Academic English Literature

appropriate management tools.

Here are some highly recommended reading and managing software: Endnote, Mendeley, NoteExpress, Notefirst, CAJViewer, Readcube, Adobe Acrobat Reader, Foxit reader, Speed PDF Reader, and so on, among which Mendeley is a free reference manager and academic social network where you can organize your research, collaborate with others online and discover the latest research.

> Tasks

❶ Download Mendeley on your computer or Mendeley APP on your phone, create a free account and get familiar with the tool before you report its major functions to the class.

_____
_____

❷ Try and compare the management tools to decide which one suits your research field most.

Your reasons:

_____
_____

4.1.2　Main Features of English Literature Management Tools

1) Functions & Services

When Zotero requires Firefox as the browser, Mendeley provides its distinctive service of collecting literature from its corporate databases, recommending literature according to your history of dealing with literature, like the fields, the topics and the authors. Endnote allows retrieving results from various databases to be imported into the personal library on it.

2) Online or Offline

Endnote and Zotero are designed for online use, which will instantly update your personal library. Reference Management and NoteExpress can be used offline. Mendeley and NoteFirst are available both online and offline, offering more convenience.

3) Free or Charged

Mendeley, Zotero, and NoteFirst offer free access to both individual users and organizations. Foreign and domestic universities usually pay for Endnote and NoteExpress, so their students and faculty can use both of them for free.

》Tasks

1 Summarize the specific features and challenges of the three management tools after using them.

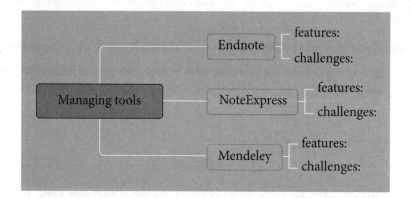

2 Introduce more literature managing tools you are familiar with.

Managing tool	Feature 1	Feature 2	Feature 3	More features

》Language Toolkit

Useful Sentence Patterns of Discussing Using Literature Managing Tools:

- Before having a further discussion about..., we need to draw a map of...
- Since it may be..., it's better to start off doing...
- Action speaks louder than words.
- A handy tool makes a handy man.
- This tool is easy to use as all the terms are offered in the menu. Thus, we only need to select a term from the drop down menu.
- To save time and avoid frustration, it's suggested to...about...
- When we fail to..., ...might be a choice.
- When ...is in vain, there is an alternative to...

> **Reflection & Practice**

1. Do you agree it's very time-consuming if we are not skillful at using the management tools?
2. Is it true with your research career that retrieving and managing academic literature accounts for more than half of the research time?
3. Browse the introductory article about management tools on the Academic WeChat platform and introduce your preferences.
4. Discuss with your group members about the features of one or two management tools you are familiar with.

4.2 Principles and Steps to Manage Academic English Documents

Classroom Voice

Bryan, after selecting a management tool, has imported the articles and other documents of the previous studies on the development of green energy into the tool. Then he started to read and manage the imported documents.

Instructor's Voice

Join Bryan to learn how to select, rank and label the imported academic literature retrieved from the digital online databases, also how to annotate the literature with highlights, summary, comments and reviews.

4.2.1 Following Some Principles to Manage Documents

Though digital retrieval and management tools are available, it's still a waste of time in the following scenarios:

- if we collect literature in a low-efficiency way, for example, download all the full texts and read them all online;
- if we store documents in disorder because of repeated downloading and forgetting where they are stored;
- if our reading purpose is to copy ideas with a vague understanding of the previous studies;
- if we insert citation and references totally manually.

To serve a specific purpose of a project or for different document genres, researchers need to consider why to collect, since it will determine which articles and what papers or similar documents are to be collected, how they are stored and annotated.

> **Tasks**

❶ Check if you have the similar problems listed above and discuss with your group on the possible reasons.

Your problems: _____

_____

_____

_____

_____

Possible reasons: _____

_____

_____

_____

_____

❷ When do you need to manage your literature? What can researchers benefit from each stage?

	Stage 1	Stage 2	Stage 3	Stage 4	Stage 5
Benefits					

4.2.2 Managing Documents in Pre-reading

There might be the cases where there are too many documents on the list though you have restricted the search items very carefully. A good document manager shall start filtering before deciding what to be imported for reading.

For an overview of a field or a topic, literature reviews in recent three to five years will be the most important ones. Articles in the coming year are suggested to be included in by extending the year to the next year, for example to cover 2021 in the year of 2020.

This will allow us to be systematically clear about what the recent achievements are, what the gap is, and what the future research can be, in terms of classical methods, latest hot spots, research trends and technical difficulties.

For a specific research topic, we can track the articles appearing in the references of the review articles. This requires a good identification ability of the documents. Usually twenty to forty articles are enough for the preliminary reading.

We can also collect the articles done by a specific author or a team who stands on the frontier and has made great achievements in the field or on a certain research subject.

Also after refining the search formula, which, to great extent, plays a critical role in ensuring a satisfactory search results in the preliminary document management, and trying different listing order (for example, relevance) several times, those articles and books that always appear on the top can be preferably selected and imported.

4.2.3 Managing Documents in Preliminary Reading

Preliminary reading aims to:

- filter one more time the documents imported into the management tool since they are highly relevant to your research (With your quick browsing of the title, the abstract, keywords and figures, until you can decide whether it can arouse your interest or it is valuable for you, the article will remain);
- have a dynamic grasp of the academic trend of a research topic by skipping the daily or weekly updates of literature.

Preliminary reading plays an important role in accumulating your research experience and professional knowledge, and expanding your academic vision. For example, EndNote has the function of organizing and grouping the references in any way that works for your research. Duplicated references can be found and deleted manually.

Then label those you have chosen as the to-read list for your in-depth reading. Divide your to-read list into two general groups of abstract reading and full-text reading, then further into more specific groups of author-based articles and keyword-based articles and review articles on your research topic and critiques reviewing the main selected articles.

4.2.4 Managing Documents in In-depth Reading

As has been advised above, the most relevant, highly cited, and the latest articles should be read very carefully, which is called in-depth reading. The introduction, the method and result in the body part, and the discussion and conclusions should be read carefully. In this stage, we had better mark the article and take notes of understanding, thoughts and problems of the article.

Notes, especially from a critical perspective, rather than a copy, can be taken on the PDF or in an electronic notebook. The latter can prepare you for your future discussion or report on the research topic, while the former can be more easily tracked for your writing. You can also use highlights in the article as shown in Figure 4.1.

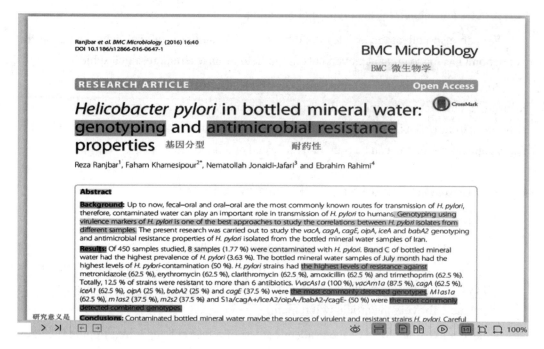

Figure 4.1　Highlights in the Article

After in-depth reading of the articles, you can spend some time sorting the articles again and rearrange and re-categorize them according to their value and relation to your research. It is also the time to know if you have obtained the articles you need to understand the research topic comprehensively. And your writing should be based on the previous literature.

4.2.5　Managing Documents in Writing

Management tools of documents can help you avoid problems with citation.

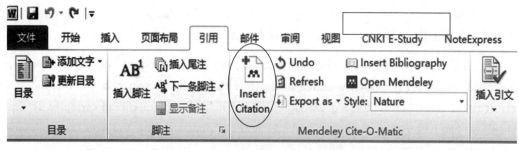

Figure 4.2　Functions of "Insert Citation" and "Insert Bibliography"

UNIT 4 Managing Academic English Literature

Managing references interrupts thoughts of writing, thus it will waste time. The formats of references are too complicated and complex to be cited in the correct form. The order of the references is likely to be disordered. The exactness of the document information like pages, publication dates may be wrong. Some frequently used English citation management tools, such as Endnote, Mendeley, Zotero, NoteExpress, Papers, ReferenceManager, Word, may be helpful.

Most tools listed above provide a sheet among various document formats when we import citations. Try "Insert Citation" and "Insert Bibliography" when using Mendeley as shown in Figure 4.2. You can enter the title or authors of the document which you want to quote in the pop-up dialog box. You must click the right citation before you hit "insert citation" and make sure you have chosen the desired citation format among a long list of various styles.

Or you can use "Cite While You Write" Plug-in via EndNote as shown in Figure 4.3. When you have a manuscript, EndNote can also help match your manuscript with journals that may be most likely to accept your writing, which will give one more opportunity to see what those journals are and what similar articles have been accepted and published.

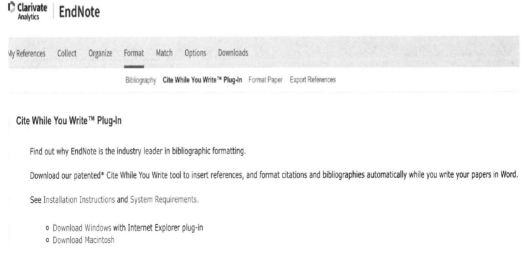

Figure 4.3 "Cite While You Write" Plug-in

4.2.6 Important Tips for Literature Management

- Literature management is always on the way. It is true for all the researchers either for regular accumulation of academic knowledge or for a specific research at hand. Deleting the unimportant articles and add those missing or new ones are based on good sense of the new findings, the gaps and contributions of the articles.
- Take useful notes. Notes are critical for researchers to understand the value of the article. Taking notes both in the literature management software and on paper

notebook is often a practical way for new researchers.

- Don't feel frustrated. All researchers are facing numerous literature. Taking a "quantity to quality" attitude may reduce your worries and build correct and accurate judgement of the academic articles.

- Build critical thinking. It's possibly a case for beginners or even for experienced researchers that they may miss the most important literature. So build critical thinking in the course of literature management, and you will gradually feel better when reading literature and rearranging them in a better way.

Tasks

1 What do you think are the advantages and challenges of managing your documents at different stages from pre-reading to writing?

Stages	Advantages	Challenges
Pre-reading		
Preliminary reading		
In-depth reading		
In writing		

2 Manage the retrieval results of your current research topic, take notes and describe orally both your literature retrieval and management.

Research topic	
Retrieval results	
Literature management	

Language Toolkit

Useful Sentence Patterns of Discussing Document Managing:

- Prior to importing the documents, we need to see their formats.
- For my research, the documents are better arranged in time sequence.
- It is...that we should consider carefully when taking each step of...

UNIT 4 Managing Academic English Literature

- It's possible to improve...if we...
- How to annotate the literature depends on...
- For...purpose, the documents are suggested to be labeled in the way of...
- Here are some techniques to...
- This is a report of my...
- The articles will be managed better if...

〉Reflection & Practice

1. Discuss about the solutions to the problems in managing documents for your current research.

2. Import the literature for one of your current research projects and manage the list of the literature in the most suitable literature management tool, then annotate some or all of the key documents for your research purpose and output the documents in the required format of references.

3. Discuss in the class or with your supervisor on how to cultivate a good sense of academic literature. See if you can make some process in managing literature more efficiently and effectively.

4. Can all the published literature be chosen as a reference? How to eliminate the coarse literature while identifying the refined ones? How to distinguish between the false ones and those with real academic values?

Unit 5
Reviewing Academic English Literature

Learning Objectives

- To recognize the importance of academic integrity and build proper academic values;

- To identify the general approaches of selecting sources to be used in your research paper;

- To explore and practise ways of organizing sources structurally and logically;

- To be able to integrate other sources into academic paper in the correct format and style.

Pre-learning Questions

1. Do you know what is plagiarism and what consequences it may lead to?
2. How to determine whether the literature you have obtained can be cited in your academic paper?
3. How to synthesize the sources into your own paper correctly and appropriately?

In most academic research papers, a review of relevant academic works in the research field is included in the introduction or written as a separate section headed "Literature Review". Apart from the separated part of reviewing literature, proper use of the authorities is expected in the whole paper to support your ideas. However, it is sometimes confusing to students when selecting relevant sources and blending them into their own writing. What is even worse is if one fails to follow the right conventions of referencing, he/she will be accused of plagiarism. In this unit, to facilitate your literature review writing, you will learn how to select sources for your own writing, the common ways of organizing sources as well as the rules of citing them.

5.1 Selecting Sources

Classroom Voice

Linda, a last-year graduate student, is working on her graduate thesis. She has collected a number of materials on her research subject from the library and the Internet, and spent several weeks reading these sources. However, she feels lost in the sources and is puzzled about what to be used in her own paper.

Instructor's Voice

Before you decide what literature is used in your own papers, it is crucial to have a clear and overall picture of what literature review is, so that you will know exactly what information you need and how to select it. Have you ever written an academic paper? Did you have the same experience as Linda has in writing?

A great number of literature related to your topic may be found, but not all of them is reliable and helpful to your study, so picking out the most relevant and useful ones should be the priority in writing a literature review. This part provides a visual and literal explanation of what literature review is and discusses the common criteria of evaluating the literature.

5.1.1 Reviewing Literature

There are many different types of literature review students may encounter or be required to write while in graduate school. Its focus may range from selective to comprehensive. It can also be part of broader work or stand alone as separated work.

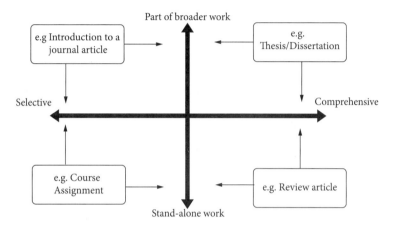

Figure 5.1 Different Types of Literature Review

Visually, Figure 5.2 and Figure 5.3 below show how the literature review differentiates from the literature. Basically, the literature is a continuously involving network of scholarly works on a topic that interact with each other, while reviewing the literature is to understand the relationships between these works and your own idea and connect them to your research.

Figure 5.2 The Literature

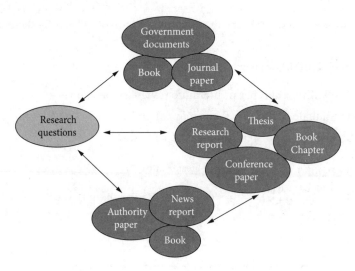

Figure 5.3   The Review of Literature

Therefore, a good literature review should show readers the current developments of the research field, critique these studies' advantages and disadvantages, and identify the gap in the field. You need to create a theoretical framework based on your research question, which includes an overview of the topic, an explanation of how publications differ from one another, and an examination of how each publication contributes to your topic. Most importantly, you also need to relate these previous works to your research by defining what the gap is in the research field and highlighting how your study will fill the gap and move the topic forward.

› Tasks

❶ Study the following example, which is from a student's review on motivation theory. Complete the theoretical framework of the theories reviewed.

The Content and Process Theories

The various theories of motivation are usually divided into content theories and process theories. The former attempt to "develop an understanding of fundamental human needs" (Cooper et al., 1992: 20). Among the most significant are Maslow's hierarchy of needs theory, McClellan's achievement theory and Herzberg's two-factor theory. The process theories deal with the actual methods of motivating workers, and include the work of Vroom, Locke and Adams.

The Content Theories

Maslow's hierarchy of needs theory first published in 1943 envisages a pyramid of needs on five levels. Each of which has to be satisfied before moving up to the next level. The first level is physiological needs such as food and drink, followed by security, love, esteem and self-fulfillment (Rollinson, 2005: 195-196). This theory was later revised by Alderfer, who reduced the needs to three: existence, relatedness and growth, and re-named it the ERG theory. In addition, he suggested that all three needs should be addressed simultaneously (Steers et al., 2004: 381). McClelland had a slightly company emphasis when he argued that individuals were primarily motivated by three principal needs: for achievement, affiliation and power (Mullins, 2006: 199).

In contrast, Herzberg suggested, on the basis of multiple interviews with engineers and accountants during the 1950s, a two-factor theory: That job satisfaction and dissatisfaction had differing roots. He claimed that the so–called hygiene factors such as the conditions and pay were likely to cause negative attitudes if inadequate, while positive attitudes came from the nature of the job itself. In other words, workers were satisfied if they found their work intrinsically interesting, but would not be motivated to work harder merely by good salaries or holiday allowances. Instead, workers needed to be given more responsibility, more authority or more challenging tasks to perform (Vroom & Deci, 1992: 252).

Herzberg's work has probably been the most influential of all the theories in this field, and is still widely used today, despite being the subject of some criticism, which will be considered later.

The Process Theories

Vroom's expectancy theory hypothesizes a link between effort and performance and motivation. It is based on the idea that an employee believes that increased effort will result in improved performance. This requires a belief that the individual will be supported by the organization in terms of training and resources (Mullins, 2006). In contrast, Locke emphasized the importance of setting clear targets to improve worker's performance in his goal theory. Setting challenging but realistic goals is necessary for increasing employee motivation: "Goal specificity, goal difficulty and goal commitment each served to enhance task performance" (Steers et al., 2004: 382). This theory has implications for the design and conduct of staff appraisal systems and for management by objective methods focusing on the achievement of agreed performance targets.

Another approach was developed by Adams in his theory of equity, based on the concept that people value fairness. He argued that employees appreciate being treated in a transparently equitable manner in comparison with other workers doing similar functions, and respond positively if this is made apparent (Mullins, 2006). This approach takes a wider view of the workplace situation than some other theories, and stresses the balance each worker calculates between "inputs" i.e. the effort made, and "outputs", which are the reward obtained.

(Source: Bailey, S. 2011. *Academic Writing: Handbook for International Students*. London & New York: Routledge, 265-266.)

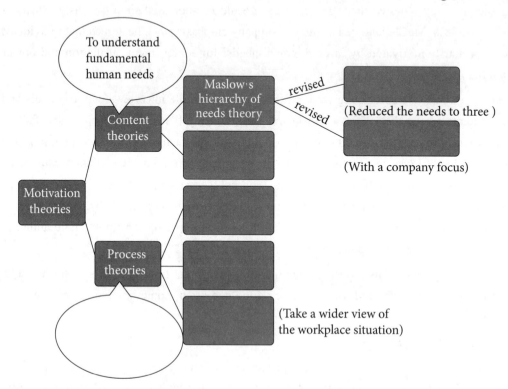

❷ **Work in small groups. Exchange your mind maps and discuss what else should be included if this is the literature review part of the student's research paper.**

5.1.2 Evaluating Sources

There is no unified approaches or rules for evaluating a source for quality and usefulness in the research. However, it is generally accepted that the following aspects should be taken into consideration: authority, accuracy, relevance, objectivity, purpose, publication, and currency.

The following table is summarized to help you remember what the standards are and what questions should be considered in evaluation.

Table 5.1 Questions About Evaluating Sources

	Questions to consider
Rationale: -To examine any personal bias the author may have	- Why was this source created? - Does it have an economic value for the author or publisher? - Does it fill any other personal, professional, or societal needs? - Who is the intended audience? - Is it for scholars or for a general audience? - What research questions does it attempt to answer? - Does it strive to be objective? Is there any bias? - Does the author omit any important facts or data that might disprove their claim? - Does the author use strong emotional language? Are there other emotional clues such as all-capitals?
Accuracy: -To distinguish the errors, untruths, and inaccurate information	- Are there statements known to be false? - Was the information reviewed by editors or subject experts before it was published? - Was it formally peer-reviewed? Or was it self-published? - Do the citations and references support the author's claim? Are the references correctly cited? - What do other people say on the topic? Is there general agreement among subject experts? - If applicable, is there a description of the research method used? Does the method seem appropriate and well-executed? - If there are pictures, were they photoshopped?
Date: -To check the currency of the information -Not always necessary	- Is the topic in an area that changes rapidly? - Is it necessary to provide a historical overview of the older literature to show how perspectives have changed? - When was the information published or last updated? - What has changed in the field of study since the publication date? - Have newer articles been published on the topic? - Is the information obsolete? - Are there any published reviews, responses or rebuttals?

(cont.)

	Questions to consider
Authority: -To judge the credibility of the author's assertions	- Who is the author? - What else has the author written? - Is the author affiliated with an educational institution or a prominent organization? - In which communities and contexts does the author have expertise? - Can information about the author be found in reference books or on the Internet? - Who was the publisher? Where, geographically, is it published? In what language? - Was it published in a scholarly publication? - Is the publisher of the information source reputable? - If it is on the Internet, is it fabricated or intended as satire?
Relevance: -To find the pertinent information to support your ideas	- How is it relevant to my research? - Does it analyze the primary sources that I am researching? - Does the information answer my research question? - What is the scope of coverage? - Is it a general overview or an in-depth analysis? - Does the scope match my own information needs? - Does the information meet the stated requirements for the assignment? - Is the information too technical or too simplified for me to use? - Does the source add something new to my knowledge of the topic? - Is the time period and geographic region relevant to my research?

UNIT 5 Reviewing Academic English Literature

> Tasks

❶ Imagine that you are writing an essay entitled "Industrial Transformation and Upgrading of Coal Industry". Read the following article and use the table followed to evaluate it.

Peabody Energy (BTU), one of the nation's largest coal miners, warned investors earlier this fall that its finances were shaky enough that there is now "substantial doubt" about its ability to stay in business. It has lost $1.7 billion in the first nine months of the year and is engaged in negotiations with lenders and bond holders to try to restructure its debt. They say that the COVID-19 pandemic and the impact on the global economy, especially manufacturing, has been a body blow for the already struggling coal industry.

The troubles for coal started well ahead of the pandemic and the recession. This week the US Energy Information Administration reported that coal production last year was down 35% from 2009, the year the economy was just crawling out of the previous recession. Total production fell to the lowest level since 1978. Coal mine utilization, which compares production to capacity, was only 70% last year, compared to the 82% average from 2010 through 2014.

Increased competition from lower-cost sources of energy, primarily natural gas, has been coal's downfall—it's not environmental regulation that's killing coal demand.

The fracking boom of recent years has not only produced more oil but it has unlocked enough natural gas to drive prices down and prompt utilities to switch from coal to gas. Falling costs for renewable energy sources such as wind and solar have also hurt.

The ongoing US-China trade dispute, which has cut demand in primary market for coal. Even though China is the one major economy to avoid a COVID-sparked recession, "Chinese imports of [Metallurgical] coal has been muted given unofficial import controls," said Peabody's Kellow.

(Source: Isidore, C. 2020. Falling sales, job losses and bankruptcies: Pain spreads across coal country. 12–09. From CNN website.)

Criteria	Negative aspects	Positive aspects
Rationale		
Accuracy		
Date		
Authority		
Relevance		

❷ Discuss in small groups. Decide whether you will refer to the article in Task 1 in your essay according to your evaluation and tell what is the most important factor that has influenced your decision. Get ready to report your discussion result in the class.

⟩ Language Toolkit

Useful Sentence Patterns of Discussing What a Literatur Review Is:

- Reviewing the literature is not to write a summary of the relevant scholarly works; rather, it should be…
- Literature is…, while literature review is…
- As far as I'm concerned, a good literature review should…
- The features of a good literature review are…
- One of the most important functions of a literature review is to…
- It is to create a theoretical framework of…Also, you should explain…More importantly, it is to…

Useful Sentence Patterns of Discussing Source Selection and Evaluation:

- Before writing the literature review, you need to fully assess the sources that are relevant to your research.
- I think many factors should be considered, for example, …
- When selecting/choosing the sources, you should critically evaluate/examine…
- When evaluating the sources, you should take a critical approach to…
- Critical thinking/reading is necessary when evaluating the precedent works.
- It is essential to distinguish/check/judge/examine/analyze…
- Many factors, such as…, should be considered/evaluated/examined/analyzed.

⟩ Reflection & Practice

1. Search and collect 3 journal articles which have a literature review at the beginning and 3 stand-alone literature review articles. Analyze the differences between these two types of literature review in content, length, scope, focus and other aspects you may notice.
2. What other factors should also be considered in evaluating sources?
3. Based on the topic of your current research direction, select 3-5 different sources using the criteria you have learned in this section or some other factors you think crucial.

UNIT 5 Reviewing Academic English Literature

Fill in the notes below and get ready to make a report in your group, explaining why you select these sources.

	Literature type & title	Why was it selected
1		
2		
3		
4		
5		

5.2 Structuring a Literature Review

Classroom Voice

Allen sent his first draft to his tutor for reviews and feedback. He was told that his literature review is not structured, and it should not be a simple list of the sources he found, so he was suggested to rewrite this part. Allen is now feeling very worried and puzzled about how to write the literature review.

Instructor's Voice

A literature review is not a simple list or unorganized summary of the relevant sources. You will need to organize your thoughts on the literature and write your review in a logical and systematic structure. However, it can be confusing to many graduate students about what to write in the literature review and how to organize the literature. In this part, you will learn the common contents of a literature review and ways of organizing different sources to clear your confusions and guide your writing.

5.2.1 Contents of a Literature Review

Generally, a literature review falls into the following contents:

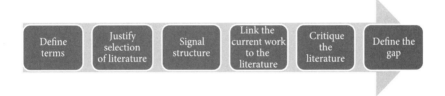

Figure 5.4 Contents of a Literature Review

1) Define Terms

Defining the key terms is to indicate which definition you are going to apply in the study, so the readers can have a basic understanding of the background knowledge. It is crucial especially when the definition is not unified or consistent.

2) Justify Selection of Literature

Indicating the selection of literature means to tell what written works you have decided to use and what are omitted, as well as the reasons for the decisions. It is to help the readers understand your criteria of selecting sources and the scope of your study.

3) Signal Structure

You should create your own theoretical framework when reviewing the literature. At this step, you are supposed to introduce the framework by telling how you have structured the precedent works.

4) Link the Current Work to the Literature

To relate the literature to the current study is an essential step. It is to demonstrate to the readers the relation between others' works and your current work. For example, the previous studies can be cited to verify the significance of your study, to support your hypothesis, method, results or conclusion, or to answer your research question(s).

5) Critique the Literature

To critique the literature is to assess the previous works and discuss their inadequacies, such as the small size of the sample, the bias of statement, the incompleteness of the study focus, and the inappropriate selection of the variables.

6) Define the Gap

Defining the gap you have spotted during your research is considered to be the most important part of a literature review. The gap means an area of a research topic that is untouched or unrecognized, or a problem of the existing research. At the end of the literature review, based on the research and discussion of the field, a conclusion should be made by stating the shortcomings or unanswered questions that are still remaining. Then, if it is part of a longer paper, a conclusion on how to fill the gap should be made as well.

UNIT 5 Reviewing Academic English Literature

> **Tasks**

1 The following extracts are taken from the literature review of some journal papers. Decide what the content is about according to what you have learned in this section.

Extract 1

Beginning in the late 1950s and throughout the following two decades, the debate on mixed-ability teaching has been given a high priority. Among the more influential writers on the subject were Rudd, Willig, Jackson, Yates, Barker-Lunn and Kelly. However, in the late 1980s there was a view abroad that "The Mixed-Ability Debate" was no longer relevant; the argument had been won and mixed-ability organisation had been accepted as the normal practice, especially in the pre-certificate stages of education. Certainly, there is a dearth of recent publications on the matter and it has been ousted from the currency of staffroom discussion by other more pressing initiatives. So, perhaps the stance has some validity. The aim of this study is not to contest this view, complacent though it may be. Rather it is the intention to maintain that if any justification does exist it is limited to the secondary and not the primary sector.

Extract 2

Different approaches were employed in these studies such as questionnaires, simulation of evacuation events and on-line survey. Japan Association for Fire Science and Engineering (JAFSE) conducted an investigation by means of questionnaire survey and peer interviews with some survivors from the fire happened on 28 October 1996 in Hiroshima City in Japan. A survey of high-rise building occupants was conducted to explore their knowledge and attitude to high-rise building safety and emergency evacuation procedures. An online survey was conducted by Kinsey to study whether occupants would use elevators for evacuation in some hypothetical situations. Most of the previous studies were conducted by online or postal questionnaire surveys. In that case, the participants might misread, misunderstand, erroneously or randomly answer the questions. On the other hand, there was no time limit for participants to answer the questions. This might lead to over-rational responses which would not happen in actual situation.

Extract 3

A Comparative Study of Two Vocabulary Learning Strategies for Chinese EFL Learners

Empirical evidence suggests that affix knowledge is important in explicit vocabulary acquisition (Mochizki & Aizawa, 2000). Schmitt and Zimmerman (2002) claimed that L2 learners had difficulties in producing the various derivational affixes with a word family. This conclusion was based on a study in which four major affixes (i.e. noun, verb, adjective and adverb) from 16 prompt words were examined in a sample of 106 graduate and undergraduate EFL students. The results showed that students had definite gaps in their affix knowledge, especially of adjective and adverb forms. This was taken to indicate a need for more explicit instruction in the derivational affixes. Mochizki and Aizawa's study of Japanese university students also conclude that intermediate and upper-intermediate learners had specific difficulties with affix acquisition. These findings were also supported by a longitudinal study of Japanese students in productive and receptive tasks, which suggested that group studied had a "weak awareness" of derivative suffixes and their use (Schmitt & Meara, 1997: 26). This again seems to suggest the importance of direct suffix knowledge instruction in second language vocabulary acquisition.

❷ **Discuss in groups on your ideas in the previous task, and explain to others how you analyze these sources and identify their contents.**

5.2.2 Ways of Grouping a Literature Review

As discussed, you are expected to group and formulate the sources when reviewing them. There are some typical ways to do so. For example, to group the literature according to their forms, the approaches they adopt, their publication date, or their subjects. Among them, the most common choices are chronological and topical method.

1) Chronological Method

If a review follows the chronological method, the sources discussed in the review should be grouped according to when they were published. By adopting this way, the readers could get an immediate understanding on how coverage of a topic changed over time. This approach is helpful for subjects where work changed considerably, such as history, sociology, education and other social sciences. However, this approach is not always effective for all subjects, especially in areas that lack continuity of development.

2) Topical Method

In this approach, the writer should break down the literature review by topic, and group them according to their different methods, focuses, findings, standings, or conclusions. For example, if your topic is to discuss the impacts of Internet chatting on communication, you can group the relevant literature according to whether they hold positive or negative attitudes towards the impacts. This approach is normally adopted in research fields where there are disagreements.

Normally, you should combine the forementioned methods in your writing. For instance, within topical organization, the chronological method could be adopted. That is, when discussing the different works within a topic, you can start with the author who first introduced that concept or conclusion, and then introduce the ideas of later researchers on the same topic in chronological order.

Writing a literature review can be puzzling to many researchers at the beginning, so if you are stuck on it, the best guide is other research papers. As discussed early in this unit, most academic papers have a literature review either as a separated section or part of the introduction. Reading and analyzing the literature review sections of the academic works in your research field could help a lot when you are deciding how to frame your own review.

Tasks

Read the texts and decide how the literature is grouped.

Text 1.

Harris (1940) in the United States found evidence to suggest that young students tended to obtain better results. Similar findings have been made in Britain by Malleson (1959), Forster (1959), Howell (1962), Barnett and Lewis (1963), McCracken (1969) and Kapur (1972), in Australia by Flecker (1959) and Sanders (1961). However, most of these studies were based on samples of students who were generally aged between seventeen and twenty-one and the correlation techniques employed meant that the relationship between age and performance really only concerned this narrow age band. As such, the results probably suggest that bright children admitted early to higher education fare better than those whose entry is delayed while they gain the necessary qualifications. This view is supported by Harris (1940) who discovered that the relationship between age and performance disappear when he controlled for intelligence. Other studies have shown that those who gain the necessary qualifications and then delay entry for a year or two are more successful than those who enter directly from school (Thomas, Beeby & Oram, 1939; Derbyshire Education Committee, 1966; Orr, 1974).

(From a review on the relationship between age and performance of study at college level.)

Text 2.

There have been studies showing that human behaviors including people's psychology, attitude and response to the environment contribute greatly to the evacuation process, e.g., pre-evacuation behaviors, and in-evacuation exit choice behavior.

(From a review on people's attitude to the use of elevator for fire escape.)

> **Language Toolkit**

Useful Sentence Patterns of Discussing How to Write a Literature Review:

- To write the literature review, you need to…
- Your review should not only cover what has been published on your topic, but should include your own thoughts and ideas.
- The sources can be organized/grouped according to…
- To review the literature, I think several steps should be followed. First, …Next, … Then, …
- To me, one of the most important things in review the literature is…
- By analyzing the literature review of other researchers, I found that …

> **Reflection & Practice**

1. Search in your research field for at least 3 academic articles that include a literature review. Analyze their literature review based on what you have learned in this section:

    1) Steps of writing the literature review: Did they follow the common steps in writing a literature review? Can you use examples from the texts to illustrate what steps they followed?

    2) Ways of organizing the review: How did they organize the literature review? Apart from the methods we introduced, did they adopt any other methods? If yes, what are they?

2. Find students in you class whose major is the same as yours and share your findings with them. Try to summarize and generalize the common contents of the literature reviews in your research field.

5.3 Citing Sources

Classroom Voice

Bob is writing his first course assignment recently. He was told by his tutor and the senior students in his school that special attention should be paid when using information from others, otherwise he may encounter severe consequences of plagiarism. He feels very anxious about plagiarism and finds it urgent to know how to cite sources properly.

Instructor's Voice

Referencing sources used in your paper is very important in academic writing for many reasons, such as to show where the idea originated, to give weights to the paper, to allow the readers to find the source, and most importantly, to avoid plagiarism.

Failing to recognize the plagiarized behaviors in your paper or failing to make reference to the sources you used in writing will lead to severe consequences in academia. Have you ever noticed the plagiarism behaviors? Can you tell some examples of plagiarized behaviors? Do you know how to make standard and correct references? This part will help you understand plagiarism and the effective ways to avoid it in academic writing.

5.3.1 Plagiarism

Basically, plagiarism means to take ideas or words, or copying from others without acknowledging their origins. It is considered as an academic crime. Therefore, it is essential to make sure anything that is not common knowledge or original is cited and referred to correctly. The following ways can be helpful to avoid plagiarism:

- understand what plagiarism is and when citations should be given;
- present the work of others as either a summary/paraphrase or a quotation (See details in Section 5.3.2);
- provide correct acknowledgement to the sources used in writing (See details in Section 5.4).

However, plagiarism is hard to define precisely and can be sometimes very accidental. Make sure you check them online or ask the tutor for advice whenever you are not sure about the case. Many university library websites offer free tutorials on how to avoid plagiarism or provide detailed explanations on cases of plagiarism behaviors.

> Tasks

❶ **Decide if the following academic situations are plagiarism or not, and explain why.**

	Situation	√ / ×
1	Cutting and pasting a short passage, with no citation.	
2	Taking a paragraph from a classmate's essay, without citation.	
3	Taking a graph from a textbook, giving the source.	
4	Taking a quotation from a book, giving a citation but not using quotation marks.	
5	Using something you think of as general knowledge.	

(cont.)

	Situation	√ / ×
6	Using a paragraph from an article that you wrote and published in the past, without citation.	
7	Using the results of your own research without citation.	
8	Giving a citation for some information but mis-spelling the author's name.	
9	Taking phrases and short lines from a journal article, changing some vocabularies, and giving citation.	
10	Using two paragraphs from an essay you wrote and marked the previous semester, without citation.	

❷ **Summarize the reasons for the plagiarism behaviors and offer some suggestions on how to avoid plagiarism.**

How did these plagiarism behaviors happen?	Suggestions

5.3.2 Summarizing, Paraphrasing and Direct Quotation

There are three ways to use words or ideas from other sources without being plagiarized: paraphrasing, summarizing and direct quotation. Normally researchers will use a mixture of these ways to incorporate the sources into their academic paper. Meanwhile, it should be noted that these ways are not confined to literature review writing. In the abstract, introduction, discussion and conclusion section, you should apply these methods to make citations.

1. Paraphrasing

Paraphrasing means to restate the original text in your own words. It is to change the wording of a text to make it significantly different from the original source without changing the meaning. An effective paraphrase should:

- have mainly different vocabulary;

- keep phrases that are in common use (e.g. the Industrial Revolution, the 19th century);
- have a different structure;
- retain the same meaning.

You can paraphrase by using synonyms, changing word class and/or changing word order. However, be careful not to use only dictionary to find synonyms, because some words may have no synonym at all. Instead, the common and professional knowledge should be used to find a replacement of the original text.

2. Summarizing

Summarizing is to condense lengthy sources into a concise form without changing the original meaning. Whereas a paraphrase will maintain all the details, a summary will include only the key information and exclude unnecessary details.

Summarizing is a flexible tool: It can be a one-sentence synopsis of an article, or a paragraph providing with details. How long it will be, how detailed it should be, and which part of the original text you want to summarize depend on the writing needs. Normally the following steps should be followed in writing a summary.

Table 5.2　Steps Followed in Writing a Summary

	Steps to follow	Purpose of doing so
1	**Read** the original text carefully and check any new or difficult vocabulary.	To understand the meaning
2	**Mark** the key points by underline or highlight.	To select the most important points/ To delete unimportant points
3	**Make notes** of the key points, and paraphrase where it's possible.	To paraphrase
4	**Write** the summary from the notes, and reorganize the structure if needed.	To paraphrase and summarize
5	**Check** the summary to ensure it is accurate and nothing important has been changed or lost.	To check accuracy and conciseness

3. Direct Quotation

Direct quotation is to use the exact words of the original text. When using direct quotations, there are several questions that should be taken into consideration carefully.

First of all, you should decide when to quote and what to quote. Select only direct quotes that make the most impact on writing—too many direct quotes will make it difficult to find your own voice. Use it occasionally only when the original text is well-known, or when it expresses an idea in a particularly concise, distinctive and interesting way that the you do not want to change or cannot change.

Then you need to consider how to integrate the original text with your own writing. Instead of dropping the entire quoted sentence into two sentences of your own, it would be better if you can show the readers how the quote fits into your idea by writing an introductory sentence or phrase, which summarizes the main idea of the quoted words or introduces the relationship between the quote and the author's arguments.

Tasks

1 Read the following text on the current media revolution and analyze the three summaries of this text.

The Death of the Paper

A hundred years ago news was exclusively provided by newspapers. There were no other ways of supplying the latest information on politics, crime, finance or sport to the millions of people who bought and read newspapers. Sometimes twice a day. Today the situation is very different. The same news is also available on television, radio and the Internet, and because of the nature of these media, can be more up-to-date than in print. For young people especially, the Internet has become the natural source of news and comment.

This development means that in many countries newspaper circulation is falling, and a loss of readers also means a fall in advertising, which is the main income for most papers. Consequently, in both Britain and the USA newspapers are closing every week. But when a local newspaper goes out of business, an important part of the community is lost. It allows debate on local issues, as well as providing a noticeboard for events such as weddings and society meetings.

All newspapers are concerned by these developments, and many have tried to find methods of increasing their sales. One approach is to focus on magazine-type articles rather than news, another is to give free gifts such as DVDs, while others have developed their own websites to provide continuous new coverage. However, as so much is now freely available online to anyone with a web browser, none of these have had a significant impact on the steady decline of paid-for-newspapers.

(Source: *Academic Writing: A Handbook for International Students*, p.44.)

UNIT 5 Reviewing Academic English Literature

Summary 1. This article introduces the process of and reasons for the newspaper's decline. Due to the free and timely nature of Internet news, people's dependence on newspapers is gradually reduced, and the newspaper industry is on the decline.

Summary 2. Newspapers used to be the only source of news for people a century ago, but recently they are facing great challenges from new sources like TV, radio and websites. Though many attempts have been made, they fail to increase the sales of newspapers again.

Summary 3. Many years ago, the latest information on politics, crime, finance or sport was provided by newspapers. For the sake of the circulation of news, newspapers are sometimes sent twice a day. Television, radio and the Internet are more up-to-date than newspapers, of which the Internet is the most up-to-date. With fewer newspaper subscribers, newspapers receive fewer ads and newspaper revenues get worse. Newspapers are important to local community, and the closure of newspapers will affect some of the activities of local communities.

Newspapers are struggling to find a way to prosper. Some of them focus on magazine articles. Some people want to save newspaper subscribers by giving small gifts. But the impact of the Internet is too big, these ways had no significant impact on the steady decline of newspapers.

1. Decide which one of these summaries is effective and explain why.
2. Study the features of the effective summary you choose and consider what makes a good summary.

❷ Work with a partner. Discuss whether you would quote, paraphrase, or not use the information in the situations below. Then share your ideas with the whole class.

A. The sentence is a famous saying.

B. The sentence contains a lot of technical terms that can't be said another way.

C. You only want to use one fact from the sentence, and not the rest of it.

D. You don't really understand what the sentence means.

E. The sentence is common knowledge.

F. The idea in the expression is extremely well expressed.

G. The idea in the sentence is important, but the sentence is long and a bit confusing.

Language Toolkit

Useful Sentence Patterns of Discussing Plagiarism:

- Plagiarism is considered as…
- It will lead to severe consequences, such as…
- Many behaviors can be considered or will lead to plagiarism, for example, …
- To avoid plagiarizing behaviors, we need to…
- Plagiarism may be caused by many reasons, including…

Useful Sentence Patterns of Discussing Definition and Ways to Paraphrase, Summarize and Quote:

- Paraphrasing is to restate/rewrite/reproduce/change the wording in your own words.
- An effective paraphrase should replace original words greatly without changing the meaning.
- Summarizing is to reduce a lengthy source into…
- To summarize the text, you should figure out the key information and exclude the unnecessary/unimportant information.
- A good summary requires…
- Quoted text/quote/quotation/direct quotation means keeping the wording and not changing anything of the original text.
- The quoted words should be enclosed in quotation marks.

Reflection & Practice

1. What plagiarized behavior do you think is accidental that students may have unintentionally? Why?
2. Find a paragraph of a scholarly work in your research field. Use the skills you have learned to:

    1) Paraphrase one sentence of the paragraph that you think is helpful to your study;

    2) Summarize the paragraph into a sentence or a shorter paragraph.

Then exchange your paraphrases and summaries with your group members, and give each other feedback on their works based on the features of a good paraphrase and summary.

5.4 Following Academic Conventions in Referencing

Classroom Voice

Alice is at the last few stages of her thesis writing on communication technology, but she found it quite time-consuming and annoying to integrate the sources into her own writing in an acceptable manner, because there are quite a lot of requirements she should follow, which she doesn't know very well. She is now eager to learn an effective way of citation and reference or some general rules she should follow.

Instructor's Voice

References provide the essential information of each work cited in your writing, which allows readers to identify and retrieve these works. Accurate and complete references not only help establish your credibility as a careful researcher, but also prevent you from plagiarism. In academic writing, there are many different referencing systems (e.g. Harvard, Vancouver) and academic writing styles (e.g. APA, MLA). Therefore, you need to be aware of which referencing system or style is generally used in your research field, and their different rules for referencing. Meanwhile, proper reporting verbs like "argue" "discuss" "indicate" "reveal" should be used to introduce the cited sources.

Do you know the referencing system or style used in your field? Do you understand their general rules when making a reference? Have you noticed the different types of reporting verbs and their different tenses? This part will introduce these general academic conventions for referencing to help you avoid plagiarism and facilitate your writing.

5.4.1 Styles of Referencing

Different referencing styles and systems are chosen because they work best for the kind of sources that are most commonly used in one discipline. You should always check which style is preferred in your disciplines or you are required to use. No matter which system is chosen, it is important to be consistent.

The four most commonly and widely used ones are the MLA (Modern Languages Association) system, the APA (American Psychological Association) system, the Harvard system, and the MHRA (Modern Humanities Research Association) system. Other styles that are used in academia are Oxford, Chicago, Vancouver and IEEE. They can be divided into 3 categories:

1) The "Name-Date" (or parenthetical) System

- The author's surname and date of publication are included in brackets in the text.
- The reference list is arranged alphabetically according to the author's surname.

e.g. The Harvard system

2) The Footnote (or Endnote) System

- Superscript numbers run consecutively through the paper and link to a sequence of notes of the sources at either the bottom of the page or the end of the paper.

e.g. MHRA system

3) The Numeric System

- Numbers in brackets are inserted after the citation and they link to a numbered list of references.
- The reference list is arranged according to when the sources are appeared in the text.

e.g. The Vancouver system

Though different referencing systems or styles vary in their forms and rules, they share the same aim of providing sufficient information to enable others to trace the works you have cited. So, two elements are essential: in-text citation and a reference list. That is, in your paper where a source is used, you should indicate the citation by telling its author and date of publication, or inserting a number. Meanwhile, at the end of the paper, a reference list which provides the full description of the sources you have cited needs to be organized alphabetically or numerically.

It is not recommended to memorize the format or rules of each referencing system and style. Rather, it is suggested to always check the format and rules of the required referencing system online or use the management tools like EndNote, Mendeley, Citavi and Zotero.

▶ Tasks

In a group of 4 or 5 students in the same major or similar majors, discuss the referencing system or style that is preferred or required in your field. Search online of its guideline and find rules for the following types of sources:

A. websites (an authored undated website article & an anonymous webpage)

B. a chapter in an edited book

C. books (one author & more than one author & editorial books)

D. e-books

E. journal articles (printed or accessed via a database)

F. conference papers (conference proceedings & individual papers with the proceeding)

G. government publications

5.4.2 Verbs of Referencing

Paraphrases, summaries and quotations are usually introduced by a reporting verb to help you integrate the cited information into your own writings. The common reporting verbs and their different tenses are summarized in the following two tables.

Table 5.3　Groups of Verbs

Group of verbs	Verbs in this group +Sentence pattern
To refer to other writers' opinions	state/observe/note/argue/suggest/claim/point out… (+ that + subject + verb)
To refer to other writers' findings	demonstrate/find/confirm/reveal/unravel/conclude/establish (+ that + subject + verb)
To identify other writers' research activity	discuss/consider/explore/describe/address/examine/deal with/concentrate on/focus on/highlight… (+ noun/noun phrase)

Table 5.4　Tense of the Reporting Verbs

Tense	When to use it
Past tense	To present the **methodology** of **single** studies.
	To present the **results** of **single** studies.
	To create academic **distance** (Indicate that the source is not current and/or to distance the current study from it).
Present tense	To generalize about **current knowledge**.
	To indicate that the author **agrees with** information or views that are being reported.
Present perfect tense	To refer to **a body of research** in an area.
	To refer to **studies** that have **been made recently**.

> Tasks

Read the sentences below and decide if the choice of tense is proper in each sentence.

1. Jones (1980) **explores** the connection between social class and accent.
2. The evidence **presented** by Watson (2004) seems to suggest that global warming is a real threat.
3. Few studies to date **examine** the effect on health of ice cream consumption.
4. In fact, as Williams **argues**, reducing alcohol consumption could be the most useful approach.
5. Clausewitz **claimed** that war was policy by another means. In effect, he **argued** that war only occurred when diplomacy broke down.
6. Kramer (1980) **found** that women earned considerably less than men for doing similar jobs.
7. In their study, Modood et al. (1996) **finds** a wide variety of identities amongst the British.
8. Johnson (1996) **analyzed** student responses to on-line learning materials.
9. Surveys **have been performed** to study the evacuees' behavior including motivation and attitude in fires.

❷ **Read the following paragraph, and evaluate its use of the reporting patterns. Discuss in groups on whether you think it is good and how you will modify it.**

Apart from accidents caused by operation against rules and command against rules, gas explosion, coal spontaneous combustion, coal dust explosion, roof accidents and flooding accidents are also common types of coal accidents that influence and restrict coal production safety. Fan examined the main reasons of the mine gas explosion accident (Fan et al., 2011). Cui discussed the types and primary characteristics of coal mine water disaster (Cui et al., 2013). Wang set up a model for coal mine water disaster emergency logistics risk assessment (Wang et al., 2012). Zhang simulated the airflow conditions dynamically when fire broke out (Zhang et al., 2012). Dong developed the optimized seismic source location (Dong et al., 2014).

UNIT **5** Reviewing Academic English Literature

❯ Language Toolkit

Useful Sentence Patterns of Introducing the Common Reference System/Style in Your Field:

- It is common practice to give credit/acknowledgement to…
- The most frequently adopted referencing system/style in my research field is…
- The referencing system is normally adopted in area of…because…
- The order of the elements, including upper and lower case and punctuation, of the reference is…
- If you need to cite…, …should be the first element of your references.
- The same rules are applied when citing…
- References to…should include the following, such as…
- …are normally cited with…, followed by…, and then…
- To make references to…, firstly, you need to put…in brackets.

❯ Reflection & Practice

1. In a group of 4 or 5 students in the same major or similar majors, collect 4-5 journal articles in your research field and analyze the following aspects:
- Their referencing system;
- The in-text citation and reference list;
- The verbs of referencing.
2. Make a group report on the analysis you made in Task 1 from the perspectives followed:
- The referencing system that is normally used in the field of your major;
- Its rules for in-text citation and reference list (Remember to illustrate the rules with examples from the journal articles.);
- The verbs of references used in the articles (Group them according to their different meanings and usages).

Part Three

Basic Academic English Communication

Unit 6
Sitting in English Academic Lectures

Learning Objectives

- To establish awareness of communication in academia;

- To grasp the related skills of note-taking in academic lectures;

- To know the access to various conference resources in your field;

- To understand the function of asking questions in Q&A session in an academic context.

Pre-learning Questions

1. What academic communication situations have you ever taken participation in?
2. Do you know typical activities that take place in conference, symposium, seminar and tutorials?
3. When sitting in English academic lectures, what will you do?
4. On what occasions do participants at an international conference talk with each other?

In this unit, you will learn how to attend academic lectures effectively. As postgraduates in any field, you must feel increasingly required to attend some academic lectures and participate in international conferences, to broaden your horizon and be active in academic exchanges. You may have chances to attend various meetings, narrow or broad in scope, such as conferences, symposia, congresses, annual meetings, forums, summits, seminars, exhibits, expositions, or other similar situations. Your benefit in attending a meeting is premised on how active and effective you are. Attending lectures and professional conferences is quite a good way to keep abreast of the latest developments in your field. The three units of Part Three are designed to help you understand the important steps for sitting in lectures, attending a meeting and performing effectively. With the necessary knowledge, practical skills and useful suggestions provided in this unit, you can make a difference and make yourself towards success in academic English communication.

6.1 Be Active Listeners

Classroom Voice

Li Ming finds his transition from an undergraduate to a postgraduate demanding. He got frustrated by his first sitting in the English academic lectures, where he caught only scraps of the lecture, and was unable to piece them together. Apart from other constraining issues, his ability to function in an English environment seems to be the most inhibiting factor to academic progress. In a lecture situation, learning to listen and listening to learn seems to be an isolated skill, not interacting with other language skills.

Instructor's Voice

It is not rare that students have difficulty in sitting in English academic lectures.

According to a series of studies on English Second Language Learning, about half of Chinese students have similar difficulty, among whom a tremendous number of students even find it hard to attend Chinese academic lectures in other academic occasions such as oral defense, panel discussion, academic presentation, conference. On this view, difficulty may derive from:

- Do you have difficulty in attending a lecture? In what aspect?
- In what way do you listen to an academic lecture? For instance, are you used to taking notes while listening?
- How much do you know about the lecture? Are you proficient in the lecture-related research area?

6.1.1 What Is Special of an Academic Lecture?

If the answers to the second question and the third one are "No", presumably you have difficulty in listening to Chinese academic lectures. Successful listening to lectures is described by Benson, a scholar in language research, as being able to "concentrate on and understand long stretches of talk without the opportunity of engaging in the facilitating functions of interactive discourse such as asking for repetitions and negotiating of meaning".

As is discussed in the previous chapters, since speech is an oral communication, its language belongs to the style of spoken language, which is different from written language. Spoken language is intended basically for ears, while written language is intended for eyes. When reading, readers can vary the speed of their reading, and if the material is complex or unfamiliar, they can slow down or even stop to reread. However, audiences cannot vary the pace of the speaker's delivery; instead, they have to follow the speaker and understand instantly when listening to a speech. Thus it is quite necessary to learn to be good listeners. Actually, good listeners must be active. They must be good at taking in the useful information they need, evaluating the information, and making quick response to the important point made by the speaker.

Whether you have ever listened to a lecture or a keynote speech, most of them are formal talks to one or more people to "present" ideas or information in a clear, structured way. The objective of a presentation is to transmit information or opinions to the audience in your own words, within a limited amount of time.

> **Tasks**

❶ Watch in class Barack Obama's national address to America's school children, and if necessary, discuss about the way the lecturer makes his presentation.

(Source: "我们为什么要上学", retrieved from bilibili website)

❷ **What are the characteristics of academic lectures the audience are supposed to be aware of?**

❸ **Work in pairs to come up with the reasons for Li Ming's problem, and make some constructive suggestions for better facilitating his listening to an academic lecture.**

6.1.2 Focusing on Language Use Strategy in Lectures

Listening to academic lectures could be defined as a problem-solving skill, in which the student plays an active and crucial role in determining not only the subject of the spoken text from the introductory words of the lecturer, but also in making correct predictions of the possible development of the spoken text. Academic listening is more than the correct matching of sounds and words, as it also involves deriving meaning from meaning-bearing words, such as conjunctions and discourse markers. Therefore, if academic success is to be achieved, postgraduates will need all available strategies to assist themselves in assimilating the information presented in oral lectures in their respective fields of study as effectively as possible.

As the speaker at an academic lecture faces and communicates with a relatively specific audience, the language and way he or she uses in speaking is usually personal and befits public speaking occasions. For example, the introduction to appropriate discourse markers will assist the lecturer in ensuring that his or her intended meaning is conveyed, as there is usually not much room provided for the negotiation of meaning in the lecture situation. In this sense, for building listening skills, listeners are encouraged to be familiar with basic characteristics of academic lectures. In addition, for the sake of impression, figures of speech, rhetorical questions and personal pronouns such as "I", "we", and "you" are often used. This style can make the audience feel more comfortable, shorten the distance between the speaker and the audience, and furthermore, increase the impact of the speech.

Figure of speech, language strategy, is an important part composing the form of spoken texts. As to spoken language, it has been dealt with in detail in Unit 1 and Unit 2 in Part One. Although figures of speech are often employed in lectures including similes, repetition, and antithesis, it is quite necessary to emphasize the language perspective in this very unit.

A **simile** is direct comparison that usually employs "like" or "as", which can provide colorful word pictures to help make speech ideas impressive and memorable. For example:

The epidemic COVID-19 is like a magic mirror of human nature.

The bottle rolls off the table like a teardrop.

Repetition, as a rhetorical device, is used to highlight certain ideas or add vividness to speaking by repeating a sound, word, or phrase, or using a series of sentences arranged in parallel structures and beginning with the same words. The speaker's repetition will help you master the content of his speech. Repetition involves starting the talk by giving the audience an overview of what the lecturer is going to say in outline form, then follow the outline, emphasize the key points and then briefly review the most important points. For example:

If you think you can do it, you can do it.

The president said, "Work, work, and work," is the key to success.

Antithesis is also used to highlight the ideas or add vividness to your speeches. It presents contrasts or opposites within the same sentence or in adjoining sentences. For example:

Know everything of something, and know something of everything.

Patience is bitter, but it has a sweet fruit.

Parallelism, which is the similar arrange of a pair or series of related words, phrases, or sentences, is regarded as the most frequently used in lectures to achieve rhythmic effect. For example:

On troop levels, there are three broadly options: "go big" "go long" or "go home", as the Pentagon has dubbed it in a review parallel for Mr. Baker's.

Limited by length and space, the language matter is presented by the following questions which are designed to assess listeners' understanding of the lecture:

- Are the speaker's ideas clearly expressed with wide, accurate usage of vocabulary and grammar?
- Is appropriate academic style with good grasp of hedging used?
- Is the choice of vocabulary appropriate for formal academic speaking?
- Do main clauses carry the important information?
- Has information been well combined (coordinated, subordinate, nominalized) in sentences?
- Have the active voice and passive voice been used appropriately?
- Do tense choices clearly distinguish between ongoing and completed events?
- Are you sure that no following errors impede your communication such as sentence fragments, dangling modifiers, ambiguous pronoun reference, problems of agreement, problems of tense, problems of articles, uncountable nouns, choppy sentences and run-on sentences?

> **Tasks**

Listen to the excerpts from Obama's national address to America's school children again, and then discuss with your group members about the following questions:

1. Pay attention to the underlined parts, what figures of speech are adopted here? Explain the role figures of speech play in lectures.
2. Refer to the above questions in the text to assess your understanding.

Now, I've given a lot of speeches about education. And <u>I've talked about</u> responsibility a lot. <u>I've talked about</u> teachers' responsibility for inspiring students and pushing you to learn. <u>I've talked about</u> your parents' responsibility for making sure you stay on track, and you get your homework done, and don't spend every waking hour in front of the TV or with the Xbox. <u>I've talked a lot about</u> your government's responsibility for setting high standards, and supporting teachers and principals, and turning around schools that aren't working, where students aren't getting the opportunities that they deserve.

But at the end of the day, we can have <u>the most dedicated teachers</u>, the most supportive parents, the best schools in the world—and <u>none of it will</u> make a difference, <u>none of it will</u> matter <u>unless</u> all of you fulfill your responsibilities, <u>unless</u> you show up to those schools, <u>unless</u> you pay attention to those teachers, <u>unless</u> you listen to your parents and grandparents and other adults and put in the hard work it takes to succeed. That's what I want to focus on today: the responsibility each of you has for your education.

I want to start with the responsibility you have to yourself. <u>Every single one of you has something</u> that you're good at. <u>Every single one of you has something</u> to offer. And you have a responsibility to yourself to discover what that is. That's the opportunity an education can provide.

6.1.3 Taking Notes

Note-taking is the practice of recording information captured from another source. By taking notes, the listener records the essence of the information, freeing their mind from having to recall everything. Notes are commonly drawn from a transient source, such as an oral discussion at a meeting, or a lecture (notes of a meeting usually are called minutes), in which case the notes may be the only record of the event. Note-taking is a form of self-discipline.

As with in reading research articles, highlighting important data and making notes can be a good way to keep track of the information as the audience move through the lecturer's process of talk. Taking notes will help you grasp what is important about the lecture. Note-taking usually includes:

- locating the main ideas as well as important sub-points;
- underlining and highlighting them;
- summarizing the ideas of the section in your own words;
- synthesizing in your notes the arguments you may question, if necessary in the Q&A session.

Note-taking is a central aspect of listening to lectures related to information management involving a range of underlying mental processes and audience's interactions with other cognitive functions. An active listener taking notes must acquire and filter the incoming sources, organize and restructure existing knowledge structures, comprehend and write down their interpretation of the information, and ultimately store and integrate the freshly possessed material. The result is information and knowledge representation helping audience to understand the lecture effectively.

Note-taking can be broadly divided into linear and nonlinear methods as follows:

1) Linear Note-taking (Outlining)

Outlines tend to proceed down a page, using headings and bullets to structure information. A common system consists of headings that use Roman numerals, letters of alphabet, and Arabic numerals at different levels.

However, this sort of structure has limitations in written form since it is difficult to go back and insert more information. Adaptive systems are used for paper-and-pen insertions, such as using the reverse side of the preceding page in a spiral notebook to make insertions. Or one can simply leave spaces in between items, to enable more material to be inserted. The above method is effective for most people, but you can be creative in making your own method.

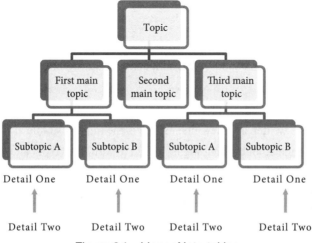

Figure 6.1 Linear Note-taking

2) Non-linear Note-taking

There are many types of non-linear note-taking techniques as shown in Figure 6.2.

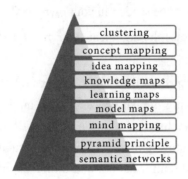

Figure 6.2 Non-linear Note-taking

Let's take the mind map for instance. Ideas are written in a tree structure (as shown in Figure 6.3), with lines connecting them together. Mind maps, also referred to as brainstorming, are commonly drawn from a central point, purpose or goal in the center of the page and then branching outward to identify all the ideas connected to that goal. Colors, small graphics and symbols are often used to help to visualize the information more easily. This note-taking method is most common among visual learners and is a core practice of many accelerated listening techniques. It is also used for planning and writing essays.

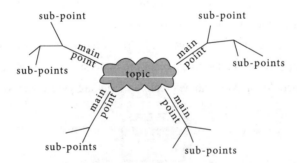

Figure 6.3 A Mind Map Connecting Ideas Together Visually

3) Sentence Method

Every new idea is written as a new line. Speed is the most desirable attribute of this method because not much thought about formatting is needed to form the layout and create enough space for more notes. When taking these notes, you can number them or bullet them. This method is demanding, but it can allow active listeners to tell where a new thought begins and ends.

4) Guided Notes

Sometimes lecturers may provide handouts of guided notes, which provide a "map" of the lecture content with key points or ideas missing. Students then fill in missing items as the lecture progresses. Guided notes may assist students in following lectures and identifying the most important ideas from a lecture. This format provides students with a framework, yet requires active listening (as opposed to providing copies of PPT slides in their entirety). Guided notes improve comprehension, recording of critical points in lecture as well as related content.

Audiences do not need to take notes like a secretary, for good note-taking is neither transcribing nor taking the speech in shorthand. As the audience, you can follow the speaker's presentation more easily by identifying the organizational pattern he employs. Organizational patterns refer to the ways that the speakers employ to elaborate their argument. The type of the presentation the speaker is giving, informative, persuasive, or explanatory, will determine the effect of audience's comprehension if they are able to distinguish what organizational patterns are employed.

5) The Value of Taking Notes of Supporting Materials

On the one hand, the speaker is developing his presentation; on the other hand, active listeners follow the train of thought. Therefore, listeners have also to identify the pattern to develop their listening or to find evidence from the speaker to support the main idea in each part. They ought to write down what the speaker processes and supports each main point through supporting materials to make it more objective, believable, and impressive. The supporting materials which are actually good guides, can be statistics, testimony, explanation, illustration, comparison and contrast, etc. to help listeners follow the main content of the lecture. What kind of supporting materials the speaker selects determines how powerful the main point is. Similarly, what notes the audience is taking goes with that.

6.1.4 Identifying Topic Sentences

Listening and reading have something in common in view of organization. First, they are the practice of language input. Second, the two share similar development in the process of a speech and an article. Most argumentations, especially those in the result and discuss section, contain a topic sentence. Identifying it helps you have a quicker understanding of the main idea of the paragraph, while the rest of the sentences merely supply details such as examples, statistics and facts to support it.

The topic sentence which generalizes the main idea of a lecture, tends to be expressed initially, lastly, and repeatedly, for this position catches the reader's/audience's attention. A conductive paragraph—a paragraph that begins with details—will have the topic sentence placed at the end of the paragraph. A long paragraph may contain a concluding sentences as well as a topic sentence. Hence looking for topic sentences is an effective way to catch ideas quickly.

Raising questions is another indication that you are an active listener. It does good to make certainty about what information you cannot get from the speaker. In the upcoming part of this unit, raising questions will be detailed.

› Tasks

❶ Listen to an academic presentation, and complete the following tasks.

1. Fill in the blanks, employing any note-taking strategy appropriate.

Thank you.

I'm thrilled to be here. I'm going to talk about a 1 _____ that still continues to amaze us, and that might impact the way we think about 2 _____, high technology, and maybe, and that might along the way, also do some stuff for medicine, and for global health and help reforestation.

So that's kind of a 3 _____. I tell you a little bit more. This material actually has some traits that make it seem almost too good to be true. It's sustainable, it's sustainable material that is processed, all in water and at room temperature, and is biodegradable with a clock, so you can watch it dissolve instantaneously in a glass of water or have it stable for years. It's implantable in the human body without causing any 4 _____. It actually gets reintegrated in the body. And it's technological, so it can do things like microelectronics, and maybe photonics do. And the material looks something like this. In fact, this material you see is 5 _____. The components of this material are just water and protein. So this material is 6 _____. So that's kind of different from what we used to thinking about silk. So the question is, how do you reinvent something that has been around for five millennia?

The process of discovery, generally, is inspired by 7 _____. And so we marvel at silk worms, the silk worm you see here spinning its fiber. This silk worm does a remarkable thing: It uses these two ingredients, 8 _____, that are in its gland, to make a material that is exceptionally tough for protein, so comparable to technical fibers like Kevlar.

(Source: Fiorenzo Omenetto's TED Talk entitled "Silk, the Ancient Material of the Future")

2. What is the title of this presentation?

_____

3. Write down the topic sentences of this lecture.

_____

_____

_____

UNIT 6 Sitting in English Academic Lectures

4) Have you benefited from the methods of taking notes? Why or why not? Report to the class.

_____

_____

❷ Discuss with your group members, and one of you will report to the class.

1. Think of a lecture, oral presentation, keynote speech that you have ever attended and the way the speaker has used to start it.

2. What will you do if you cannot follow the speaker?

3. What kind of academic lecture is regarded as good? What kind of speakers are popular with the audience?

〉 Language Toolkit

1) Useful Sentence Patterns of Emphasizing/Omitting Used in the Presentation

- Since this is a key problem, I'd like to go into some detail.
- Please allow me to deal with this matter more extensively.
- For the sake of time/In the interest of time/Because of my time is running short/Limited by the time available, I will talk about this subject briefly.
- I will not go over all the details, suffice it to say that the conclusion is reliable.

2) Useful Sentence Patterns of Changing (Sub) topics

- The second theme I want to touch on briefly is…
- Let me briefly mention some of the key steps and issues that have led to the creation of frozen light pulses.
- Before concluding, I would like to touch on one other important change that I believe would enhance…

〉 Reflection & Practice

1. What else can you do to be an active listener?

2. Interview your group members how they deal with their listening problems, and share your problem and solution.

3. Attend an academic lecture, employing the strategies of note-taking discussed in this part.

4. What can be done to improve your intake of the professional and linguistic elements in attending English academic lectures?

6.2 Evaluating While Listening

Classroom Voice

Li Na got an overall band of 6.5 in the IELTS, with the score of 7.5 for listening. She did not feel listening to lectures was too hard before. Yet, last month, she traveled to Beijing for a professional conference in new material, where five keynote speeches and other oral presentations were delivered by experts. One the one hand, there she took notes rich in information, she really found enormous benefits for a broader perspective of her field; and on the other hand, she found it hard to piece the information together for global understanding. She realized she is not an active listener because she failed to understand half of the lectures. She was busy with taking important notes without evaluating the speeches while listening, for the purpose of better understanding and thinking. Once back to school, Li Na asked her supervisor for advice.

Instructor's Voice

Li Na's puzzles actually involve the speaker's role and audience's role respectively. Having got the sense for speaker's part, both you and Li Na should attend more lectures in the specific field if necessary. When taking notes, Li Na stood no chance of getting the point of the lectures, even losing the logical thread. Therefore, if you want to achieve a good sense of understanding an English lecture, learn to lay the groundwork for the forthcoming lecture, which is equally necessary. Preparation involves referring to its background, predicting what methodology the lecturer will employ, what findings he/she will have got, and so on, from the perspective of listeners. In other words, try to evaluate the lecture's idea development and check whether the lecturer finally answers their questions of preposition.

The length of an academic presentation, for example, varies from less than ten minutes to more than one hour and it is impossible for you to take notes from the beginning to the end. A better approach is to focus on one or two major points and some significant supporting ideas. In this sense, evaluating is the important step in attending academic lectures. What are you going to evaluate? In this existing context, concentrate on:

- the information conveyed by the lecturer;
- the information received by the audience.

Evaluating, two-way communication, suggests whether the speaker is competent, and also whether you are an active listener or not. Although the speaker has rehearsed his or her presentation for several times before standing on stage, he or she has to make adjustments in the lecture on the basis of the reaction from the audience. Likewise, audience can evaluate the speaker themselves, and the significance of the lecture. It is about searching academic abilities including basic grammatical, professional, logical reasoning, critical and thinking ability, etc. to make sure whether the speech is beneficial to your sitting, whether your comprehension is satisfactory in the related topic.

Here are some indexes of questions (taking the case of engineering research) for your reference to assess academic lectures.

These questions in Figure 6.4 maps show the general view for audience to evaluate whether the main points conveyed by the speaker are actually developed logically, which helps test whether the listeners themselves can follow the speaker. The table below provides some other specific questions about each section such as the introduction, body, discussion and conclusion, help the audience further their evaluation of the lecture's significance, of the lecturer's presentation ability, and of how much the listener can understand.

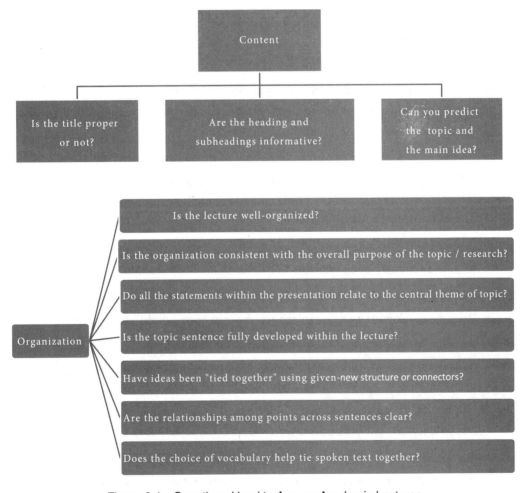

Figure 6.4 Questions Used to Assess Academic Lectures

1) The Introduction Section

- Does the speech address the topic directly or introduce the necessary context for the topic?
- Is the purpose of the topic/research clearly stated at the outset?
- Has the need for this topic/research been clearly established?
- Is the general purpose and justification for the topic/research clear to the non-specialist?
- Is the topic/research clearly and explicitly stated? And are the questions answerable and manageable?
- Are similarities and differences of previous studies pointed out?

2) The Body Section

- Does the speaker divide the body section into several parts with a clear heading marker for each part?
- Are these headings logically linked and expressed?
- Does it include sufficient information about the participants, instruments, data-collection and data-analysis so that the reader/audience can duplicate the speaker's study if they like?
- Are the results clearly reported with the help of figures and tables if possible?
- Are the figures and tables self-evident without reading the text?

3) The Discussion/Conclusion Section

- Is the topic/research question fully answered?
- Is there a summary of chief points illustrated in the body section?
- Does the speaker compare his or her results with those of previous studies?
- Does the speaker offer some explanation for unexpected or different results?
- Does the speaker point out the implication of his studies?
- Does the speaker mention some limitations and directions for further studies?

4) Use of Sources

- Does the lecturer use outside sources to support his or her ideas and argument?
- Is it evident why all the sources have been cited?
- Have all the sources been adequately, consistently and correctly in-lecture referred to?
- Does the speaker synthesize well from several sources by using appropriate reporting verbs?

UNIT **6** Sitting in English Academic Lectures

- Are all the sources the speaker used in the lecture listed in full detail in the references?
- Does each citation in the reference include the author, title, date and place of publication and sometimes page numbers?

As regard to the above indexes of questions employed in assessing an academic presentation, they are equally necessary and important for evaluation of academic paper reading.

〉Tasks

❶ Listen to the TED Talk entitled "Visualizing the Wonder of a Living Cell" in class, and then complete the following tasks.

1. Try to identify the key points.

Point One:

Point Two:

Point Three:

2. In the meantime, you are required to evaluate the lecture by asking yourself the following questions.

1) What is the content?

_____

2) What is the organization?

_____

3) What is the introduction?

_____

4) What is the body?

_____

5) What is the conclusion?

_____

(Source: David Bolinsky's TED Talk entitled "Visualizing the Wonder of a Living Cell")

❷ Discuss with your group members about the following questions.

1. What kind of lectures do you think is acceptable to the audience?
2. What are we required to do before and during the lecture?

Language Toolkit

1) Useful Sentence Patterns of Quotation and Illustration Used in a Lecture

- And to conclude, I quote the Guru once again: Education should retrieve science from lending itself to unscrupulous ways that are destructive to mankind.
- The evidence in my findings seems to support…
- I take just one of his figures to illustrate my point.
- On a positive note, it seems that…, according to my findings, as evidenced in one of the questions that I asked.

2) Useful Sentence Patterns of Summarization

- I have drawn together the threads of argument in this long discourse.
- This concludes my presentation, and I would be pleased to answer any questions you may have.
- Before closing my presentation, I would like to make a few general remarks about the problem we are discussing. I hope you will give me your comments and suggestions. Thank you!
- So, I would like to finish with a proposal…

Reflection & Practice

1. Each member in your group is encouraged to make preparations for delivering a mock academic lecture on a topic in your fields respectively. Then work in groups and talk about the way you evaluate a lecture, from both the audience's and the speaker's perspectives. Then report to the class.

2. Attend an academic presentation together with the students who are majoring in the same as you, and try out to identify the main idea sentences. Then share with the members in your group, and you will find different topic sentences will be proposed. Why is that?

3. Observe one professor in your field and your group members, and find how they act when sitting in lectures.

4. Make a comparison of your professor's and your classmates' good practice, and learn from them.

6.3 Raising Questions for Further Understanding

Classroom Voice

Jingjing, a first year graduate student, attended a lecture last week. She was happy and excited to be given a chance to ask the lecturer two questions. From the speaker's answer, she gained further insight into one concept beyond her understanding. Recently, she is wondering about a question: "Being active does not mean only to act actively as simply a listener." What else can she do to facilitate her academic progress in attending lectures?

Instructor's Voice

Both the speaker and the audience want to perform well in the discussion, you'd better be prepared for (even rehearse) the Q&A session. To some degree, it is a greater challenge for the presenter.

Jingjing's progress shows she is aware of communication with the lecturer by raising questions. The Q&A session serves for a platform for academic exchange between lecture participants involved. Therefore, you are supposed to attach importance to this procedure.

6.3.1 Functions of Asking Questions

Sitting in a lecture, the atmosphere of idea exchange is indispensable. Lectures call for mutual communication between the information-sender and information-receiver. Regardless of a lecture or a presentation, it involves two parties: the speaker, and the audience.

Communication is characterized with on-the-spot interaction. Raising questions is an indication that you are an active listener, as well as an implication that you are academic communication-conscious. Asking questions can serve a lot of functions, for example:

- to obtain an answer;
- to gain possible solutions to a problem;
- or just to signal your presence, etc.

As a questioner from audience, you should write down your questions and think about why you ask them. Your questions should be relevant to the topic of the presentation. There are two tips for the audience when asking questions: (1) Speak loudly so that you won't be asked by the lecturer to repeat that question; (2) Make the question short, simple and to the point. You are asking a question rather than expressing your opinion which can be saved until the end of the lecture.

Questions are raised usually in steps as follows:

1) Signaling your intention

If you want to ask a question, you should raise your hand. If you are picked by the presenter or the chairperson, you then announce your intention to ask a question. For example:

- I want to ask Dr. Green a question.
- I have a question for Dr. Leach.
- There is a question I'd like to ask Prof. Benjamin.

2) Expressing your attitude

Before asking your question, you can express a positive attitude or make a comment on the speaker's presentation. For example:

- Dr. Pinson, I was fascinated by your description of your study, but what will happen if…?
- Mr. Green, you did splendid work! Just one question.

3) Asking a specific question

Then you may put forward the specific questions. The following expressions might be helpful in asking questions:

- You mentioned very briefly that you used two experiments that were the same. Would you please elaborate on that point?
- Would you be so kind as to give more information about the method of your experiment?
- I don't quite understand what you really mean by saying "…". Can you explain it again?

› Tasks

❶ Work in groups to discuss what other functions of Q&A session you can think of, besides those mentioned above.

❷ Have you ever posed any questions to the lecturer? Share your experience.

❸ Work with your partner to discuss the following questions:

1. Why do most speakers feel it difficult to conduct an oral defense?
2. Are questions for lectures predictable? Why or why not?
3. What are the features of on-the-spot questions?

6.3.2 Purposes of Asking Questions

During the lecture in Q&A session (or an oral defense), the audience may raise various kinds of questions out of different motivations.

According to the audience' motivation, their questions could be categorized into the following types: (1) questions for clarifying problems; (2) questions for showing special interest; and (3) questions for raising different opinions.

The discussion session provides the audience with an opportunity to clarify the points that they have not quite understood or that have not been fully demonstrated, to ask for some statistical information, etc.

1) Questions for Clarifying Problems

- I don't quite understand what you really mean by saying that…Can you explain it again?
- I would be glad if you could give definitions to the essential concept of A used in your presentation, for I am curious why you used them in this way in your report.

Clarifying questions could be labeled as "ordinary questions". In the Q&A session at a conference, these ordinary questions usually make up the greatest proportion.

2) Questions for Showing Special Interest

- I am very interested in the subject of your lecture. If I am not mistaken, I remember that you used the abbreviation COVID-19. To the best of my knowledge, I understand it has slightly different implication if it is compared with the very approach described in your written paper published in a recent issue of *Science*. Could you explain it a little more explicitly?

Questions showing special interest in the lecture differ from the first category in that the purpose of the first category of question-raisers is mainly to have a few points clarified, whereas the second category is to satisfy certain special interest.

3) Questions for Raising Different Opinions

- I agree with you about the approaches to solving this problem. But so far as the application aspect is concerned, I'm afraid I can't say that I go along with you on that. According to the result of the experiment we made last year, I think… I would like to hear your opinion on this matter.

It is not rare that professional insiders will ask questions for expressing different opinions, and even finding what is inappropriate delivered by the lecturers. Scientific research tends to lead to different conclusions, opinions or viewpoints. Therefore, it is quite natural to find different opinions in professional discussion sessions.

This type of questions are raised when someone in the audience disagrees with the opinions, ideas, description, and explanation made by the presenter. They are normally raised in a polite and roundabout way. The questioners adopt an appropriate tone and words so as to avoid unpleasant feelings.

Language Toolkit

Useful Sentence Patterns of Raising Different Opinions:

- I don't quite understand what you really mean by saying that…Can you explain it again?
- I'm very keen on your mentioning about the…How is it being carried out in your laboratory? What do you mean by…, and how do you think it can be tackled?
- In your presentation, you mentioned ABC which is also the subject we've been groping for.
- I am very glad that I got some sidelights from your views. But as you're talking about…, I'm afraid at least the following case seems to have been overlooked. First… Second…What do you think of it?
- I am not an expert in this area. But I'm afraid there are other problems connected with the subject, which have not been mentioned in your presentation. Here are some relevant examples. Can I have your comments on that?
- Maybe I missed the point, but I don't know whether Mr. Freud is correct about this…
- Now I'd like to raise a different question… I would like to know a justification in details.

Tasks

❶ Suppose you are a questioner, how would you raise questions to a lecturer? How would you raise a question of clarification? How would you show special interest to an idea?

❷ Work with your group members. First, each chooses one topic and makes an oral composition about it. Then, suppose all of you have finished a presentation on the chosen topic. Try to raise questions for different purposes discussed in this unit, and make your response to the questioners on the speaker's part.

UNIT 6 Sitting in English Academic Lectures

> Reflection & Practice

1. Interview a lecturer of international conferences or other formal professional discussions. Find whether he/she has been asked any rebuking questions or sensitive questions. And if the answer is yes, how did he/she deal with them?

2. The lecture live is dynamic. Think of several other cases in which typical questions are dealt with, for example, if you want to follow up others' questions or shift the topic. In this situation, how should you perform?

Unit 7
Asking and Answering Academic Questions

📝 Learning Objectives

- To know reasons for asking questions and the different types of questions;

- To learn the appropriate language expressions of asking and answering questions;

- To improve the effectiveness of asking questions and the skills of dealing with questions;

- To understand the culture differences and the etiquette of asking and answering questions in cross-culture communications.

Pre-learning Questions

1. Why do people ask questions in academic communication?
2. How do you ask questions for different purposes properly and politely?
3. How do you deal with questions, especially tough and tricky questions, with a proper manner?

Asking and answering questions is an indispensable part of academic communication. It can benefit both the questioner and the answerer in many aspects. To ask questions in public can be stressful and requires certain skills, while dealing with questions, especially the tricky and difficult ones, is rather stressful and requires not only one's professional knowledge but appropriate techniques. Culture differences and the common etiquette of international communication should also be considered. In this unit, you will learn the different forms of questions, practise the related skills as well as the etiquette of asking and answering questions.

7.1 Understanding Questions

Classroom Voice

Elton is going to attend a presentation session at an academic conference as one of the keynote speakers, and he is informed to get ready for answering questions in a Q&A session at the end of the session. He feels under great pressure to deal with the questions he might be asked.

Instructor's Voice

There are many cases when you will ask or answer questions, for example, in a lecture, seminar discussion, the Q&A of a presentation session or even a private conversation with other researchers. The questions in different occasions differ in their features and difficulties. Questions in the Q&A of a presentation are considered to be the most challenging ones and cause stress to presenters, even the experienced presenters.

Have you experienced the same pressure as Elton does before presentations? What are the difficulties you had in answering questions in the Q&A? Why do the Q&A cause pressure and anxiety? This part will help you understand these questions at a deeper level.

UNIT 7 Asking and Answering Academic Questions

7.1.1 Reasons for Asking Questions

Asking questions in academic situations has many advantages for both the questioners and the answerers. For questioners, by asking questions they can gain knowledge, obtain additional information, clarify unclear points, check comprehension, show interests in the subject or challenge others' ideas. For answerers, dealing questions properly allows them to reinforce audience's impressions of their ideas, receive valuable feedback on their studies, show research capabilities, encourage exchanges of ideas, and promote new thoughts or future cooperation.

› Tasks

❶ Discuss in groups on one of your particular experiences of asking or answering questions. Tell your group the details of your experience, including the following questions. And explain how the experience benefits you or your study. After you finish your talk, your group members should ask at least a question according to your experience, and you will need to answer their questions. Then change your role.

- when it was;
- what the occasion was;
- whether you were a questioner or the answerer;
- what kind of question it was;
- why you asked or why your questioner asked the question;
…

❷ Think of why you asked the questions in the discussion in Task 1, and notice if you have some other reasons for asking questions. Note down what you learnt or what problems you had in the process of asking and answering questions.

7.1.2 Questioning in Q&A Session

Questions in the Q&A section of a presentation are relatively formal and different from those in a discussion. Many presenters feel resistant, anxious, and even frightened of the Q&A session due to the difficulties of these questions.

Generally, the questioners are experts or researchers in the related fields who know the topic well. Their questions, therefore, can be very professional, insightful or sometimes even "nit-picking". They are very likely to find the mistakes or weak points made in the presentation, so the questions they raise can be very difficult and thorny to deal with.

Another major reason is the features of the "on-the-spot" questions. Table 7.1 summarizes these features and the difficulties they cause.

Table 7.1 Features of Questions in Q&A and Difficulties It Causes

Features of the questions in Q&A	Difficulties it causes
Extensiveness	➢ Wide coverage of topics, ranging from: 　- General to detailed; 　- Theoretical to practical; 　- Present to future; 　- Non-professional to technical. ➢ Heavy task of preparation.
Unpredictability	➢ No logical or systematic relations among questions; ➢ Impossible to make any advanced preparation of the answers; ➢ Surprising questions maybe asked.
Instantaneity	➢ Immediate responses are required; ➢ Harsh demand of professional knowledge, language ability and techniques.

As for the questioners, pressure will also be felt when asking a question, especially when their questions are not understood by the presenter. To avoid it, remember to ask the question once at a time, keep the words simple and short, follow the common steps of questioning, and master the relevant techniques. (See details in Section 7.2)

❯ Tasks

❶ Discuss in groups about any other possible reasons that lead to the difficulties of the Q & A session and provide some suggestions on dealing with these difficulties.

❷ Based on discussion in Task 1, complete the table (You can add extra lines if necessary). Then introduce your table in class.

UNIT 7 Asking and Answering Academic Questions

Reasons	Difficulties it causes	Suggestions

Extensiveness	➢ Wide coverage of topics:
	  - General to detailed;
	  - Theoretical to practical;
	  - Present to future;
	  - Non-professional to technical.
	➢ Heavy task of preparation.
		➢

Unpredictability	➢ No logical or systematic relation among questions; ➢ No possibility of any advanced preparation of the answers; ➢ Surprising questions.	➢
Instantaneity	➢ Immediate responses; ➢ Harsh demand of professional knowledge, language ability and techniques.	➢

〉 Language Toolkit

Useful Sentence Patterns of Discussing the Reasons for Asking and Answering Questions:

- Asking and answering questions benefits researchers in many aspects…
- The rationales behind asking and answering questions are…
- There are several reasons that lead to/cause…
- Asking questions allows researchers to…
- The questions in Q&A session have many features including…
- The questions may be very diverse and cover a wide range within your presentation topic
- To deal with the problem of…, it is important to…

- It would be helpful if you can…
- To get ready for the Q&A, you have to do a lot of preparation work such as…
- Since the questions are extensive, …
- In the Q&A session, you are expected to answer the questions immediately, so…
- Apart from having a good command of professional and technical knowledge, …

》Reflection & Practice

1. Are questions in a presentation predictable and able to be prepared? Why or why not?
2. Which feature of the questions in the Q&A session you worry about most? Why?
3. In what cases will you ask a question? Do you find asking questions stressful? Why?

7.2 Asking Questions

Classroom Voice

Fiona has attended a conference presentation session recently. She was interested in the sample selection in a presentation and wanted to learn more details. In the Q&A of the presentation, she asked a question on it, but failed to get the answer she wanted, which made her feel very disappointed.

Instructor's Voice

Asking questions, especially in public occasions, can be stressful for the questioner. If the question fails to be organized in a clear and easy-to-follow way, many troubles may be found. One of the most common problems is failing to get the answer you want, just like what Fiona encountered. So, you need to follow the general way of asking a question to help the presenter follow your talk, realize the purpose of the question and give you the answer you expect. In this unit, you will learn the common template of asking a question and the different types of questions to help you ask questions more effectively.

7.2.1 Template of Asking a Question

In a formal Q&A session, normally when asking a question, you need to raise your hand up and make a self-introduction to help the presenter see where you are and know your background, especially professional background like the affiliation and research area, so that the presenter can recognize the focus of your question more easily, which, in turn, will help you get the answer expected.

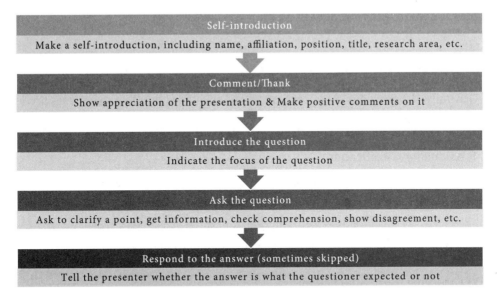

Figure 7.1   Steps of Asking a Question

Another convention is to make comments on the presentation or appreciate the efforts made by the presenter before asking the question. It is to create a good relationship between you and the presenter without being too aggressive.

Also, in order to help the presenter understand the focus of your question, you should introduce the question by indicating which part or which point of the presentation it concerns with. For example, you can introduce the question by saying "I got a question about the first point you had in the last section of your presentation".

Finally, after the question is answered, a common etiquette is to respond to or appreciate the answer. Sometimes you can raise follow-up questions if you find the answer unsatisfied or want to learn more. However, due to time limit in some cases, this step may be skipped.

〉Tasks

❶ **Watch a video of a lecture on the revolution of mass communication and take some notes. Prepare at least one question according to the contents.**

(Source: "Lecture Ready 1", retrieved from bilibili website)

❷ Work in groups and ask the question you prepared in Task 1 following the template of asking a question. Then check other group members' understanding of your question and ask their feedback on it.

7.2.2 Types of Questions

Generally, the questions at the conference can be divided into four main types according to their different purposes.

1) Asking for Clarification

This is probably the most common question type in the Q&A. One of the purposes of the Q&A is to provide the audience another opportunity to clarify the points they don't understand or fail to catch. By raising this type of question, questioners can get a repetition, elaboration or explanation from the presenter, so that the unclear point can be clarified.

2) Exploring More Information

Questioners may also ask questions to learn more on a particular aspect of information they are interested in. These questions will help them get an answer with more details or gain a deeper level of understanding.

3) Checking Comprehension

To ask this type of question, questioners needs to tell their own understanding on a certain point of the presentation first, and then ask the presenter to check if the understanding is correct or not. It can be helpful to clarify misunderstandings and ensure the accuracy of notes.

4) Challenging an Idea

In academic world, it is normal to have different opinions, standpoints, ideas, or conclusions, so it is very common to find different opinions on the presentation. Questioners can also show their disagreement with the presenter's ideas by asking this type of questions. However, it is important not to make them too aggressive. Make sure it is raised in a polite and roundabout way by adopting a mild tone and appropriate words.

UNIT 7　Asking and Answering Academic Questions

> **Tasks**

❶ Work with a partner. Check the appropriateness of the following questions and comments. Discuss which ones are not appropriate and why. Then classify the questions according their different types.

A. Could you please repeat your second main point?

B. I don't think what you said about the factors that influence the environment is correct. Actually, I'm a professional environmentalist, and in my study…Do you think so?

C. What song was playing during your presentation? Could I borrow the record?

D. You were supposed to talk for 20 minutes, but you speak for 25 minutes. Can you explain why?

E. Can you show that slide of the line graph again? I didn't understand what it was showing.

F. In the last section of your presentation, you mentioned that the safety precautions in underground mines can be generalized in other mines. Do you mean they are also helpful in open-pit mines?

G. How long did it take you to draw the graph?

H. Have you stopped drinking so much coffee since you learnt this information?

I. How didn't you quote any expert in your presentation?

J. I'm not sure about what you really mean by saying that this theory is not always infallible. Can you explain it again?

K. I'm very interested in your experiment. I wonder if you could tell us more details about it.

❷ Use the notes you made in Task 1 of Section 7.2.1. Try to ask different types of questions and write them in the table below. Work in groups and take turns to ask all the questions you prepared one at a time in a random order without telling others which type of question it is. Then write down other students' questions in the right place of the table.

Types of questions	Your question	Other students' questions
Asking for clarification		
Exploring more information		

(cont.)

Types of questions	Your question	Other students' questions
Checking comprehension		
Challenging an idea		

❸ Check their understandings of your questions in Task 2 to see if they have put your questions in the right place in the table. Ask their feedback on your questions and think about how to improve them.

❯ Language Toolkit

Useful Sentence Patterns of Asking Questions:

1) Self-introduction

- Good morning/afternoon/evening, Mr./Ms.…
- My name is…, from…
- My research area is…
- I'm doing/working on…recently/these days.

2) Making Comments

- Thank you for your enlightening presentation.
- Your presentation is very informative, and I have learnt a lot from it.
- Your presentation is truly an eye-opener.
- I'd like to express my great appreciation/gratitude to your effort in making the presentation.

3) Introducing the Question

- I have a question about X point of X part/section/slide about…
- I am very interested in…when you were introducing…
- I'm very keen on what you said about…
- X you mentioned is (greatly) related to my research/study/project.

4) Responding to the Answer

- Yes, I see.
- OK, thanks.
- Thanks, that's clear now.
- Well, thank you (for your kind explanation/vivid examples…)
- I'm afraid that's not what I was asking. What I mean was…
- Ok, but what I really wanted to know was…
- Perhaps I didn't make my question clear. What I was really asking was…
- Sorry, I'm still not clear about…
- I really appreciate your answer, but I still doubt the point you made about…

Useful Sentence Patterns of Asking Different Types of Questions:

1) Asking for Clarification

- I'm sorry I didn't follow what you said about…
- I don't quite understand what you really mean by saying…
- What did you mean when you said…?
- Could you give me an example of…?
- Can you explain…again?
- Could you please tell me…?
- Could you explain that again, please?
- Is it possible for you to illustrate…with several practical examples?

2) Exploring More Information

- Could you tell us more about…?
- Could you expand a bit on what you were saying about…?
- Would you please say a few more words about…?
- I wonder if you could tell us more details about…?
- Would you mind giving some suggestions on…?

3) Checking Comprehension

- So, you mean…?
- So, you're saying…?
- Can I just check what I've understood—did you say…?
- Have I got this right…?

4) Challenging an Idea

- I've got some insights from your views. But as to your saying about…
- It seems to be a little bit overlooked/overstated/unreliable/unreasonable…Can you make some comments on this?
- Perhaps we're looking at the problem from different viewpoints. To the best of my knowledge, what you say seems to be…Can I have your comments on that?
- I'm of the opinion that…But so far as…is concerned, I'm afraid I can't say that I go along with you on that. And I would like to hear your explanation about that.
- Would you please give us some explanation about this?

> **Reflection & Practice**

1. Which types of questions do you think are relatively easier to answer? What questions are rather difficult for you? Why?

2. Work in small groups of 4 or 5 students to discuss the greatest problems you found in asking questions and possible ways to solve them. Each student is supposed to speak for 1 minute. After each one has spoken, the others in the group should ask at least one question individually. Practise the template of asking questions and try to ask as many different types of questions as possible using the language expressions above.

7.3 Answering Questions

Classroom Voice

Jackson is required to make a presentation on his thesis proposal, and he is supposed to answer his supervisor's and other students' questions in the Q&A session at the end of his presentation. Although he is confident with the presentation delivery, he is extremely anxious that he may make mistakes in the Q&A session and can't answer all the questions.

Instructor's Voice

Answering questions in the Q&A session requires many abilities of the presenter, including professional knowledge, language proficiency, understanding of questions, utilization of skills, experiences, awareness of cultural differences, etc. Even though you are confident with your professional knowledge, you may feel worried as most presenters do. As discussed earlier in this unit, questions in the Q&A session are difficult due to their features like unpredictability, extensiveness and instantaneity, so the questions sometimes can be thorny to cope with.

There are no infallible methods to be used in dealing with all kinds of questions in all cases. However, you can familiarize yourself with the general skills for answering questions, the ways to answer normal questions and the skills to deal with difficult questions, so that you could survive in the Q&A session. In this part, these skills will be introduced and you will have chances to practise them.

7.3.1 General Skills for Answering Questions

The problems presenters may encounter at each stage of answering and the skills needed to deal with the problems are summarized in Table 7.2.

Table 7.2 Problems Presenters May Have and Skills Needed

Stage of answering	Problems presenters may have	Skills needed
Understanding the question	- Fail to hear the question	- Listen carefully - Ask the questioner to repeat
	- The question may have an implicit meaning	- Have second thoughts - Analyze the real motivation, attitude, connotation and inquiry
	- Uncertainty about the understanding on the question	- Check the comprehension with the questioner
Thinking about the question	- No time to think	- Play for time (use delaying expression)
Answering the question	- Don't know the answer	- Be honest
	- Don't know how to organize the language	- Copy the original question pattern
	- Don't know how to explain	- Refer back to related contents of the presentation
	- Be asked several questions at one time	- Deal with questions one at a time - Answer questions partially
	- The answer sounds too arrogant	- Adopt hedging expression
Checking the answer	- No responses from the questioner	- Check with the questioner for satisfaction

Apart from the skills above, presenters should always mind their manners when dealing with the questions. Both politeness and seriousness are expected in the whole process. Here are some suggestions:

- pay special attention to the body language (e.g. look at the questioners and keep smiling while they are speaking);
- welcome the questions by saying thanks or making positive comments;
- don't stop the audience and wait patiently until they finish their questions;
- be considerate for the audience (e.g. use euphemism to "unpleasant" questions);
- don't be too confident or arrogant (e.g. use hedging expressions).

Also, presenters should be aware of the culture differences, especially when dealing with questions at international conferences. Topics related to some sensitive issues like religion, convention, and cultural values should be dealt with carefully. Besides, the way how people ask questions may vary greatly in different countries as well. For example, in most English-speaking countries, people tend to tell their opinion straightforwardly and ask questions directly, while in many Asian countries, people like to talk in a roundabout way. Therefore, the real motivations of their questions need to be considered before answering.

Tasks

1 Discuss in groups on the importance and necessity of each stage of answering. Think about it with your experiences of answering question in a Q&A. Summarize your ideas and complete the second column in the table below.

Stage of answering	Importance of the stage	Problems presenters may have	Expressions
Understanding the question		- Fail to hear the question	
		- The question may have an implicit meaning	
		- Uncertainty about the understanding on the question	
Thinking about the question		- No time to think	
Answering the question		- Don't know the answer	

UNIT 7 Asking and Answering Academic Questions

(cont.)

Stage of answering	Importance of the stage	Problems presenters may have	Expressions
Answering the question		- Don't know how to organize the language	
		- Don't know how to explain	
		- Be asked several questions at one time	
		- The answer sounds too arrogant	
Checking the answer		- No responses from the questioner	

❷ **Write 2 or 3 different language expressions for dealing with the problems in the table above. Then exchange your ideas with other students in your group, and complement your table.**

7.3.2 Direct Answers

If presenters know the answer to a question, they can offer the fact or tell the opinion directly. Normally, there is no special language patterns or techniques that need be adopted. However, a 3-step-answering template which is helpful in structuring the answer logically and rationally into a speech is often adopted by many presenters.

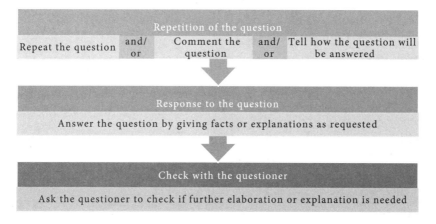

Figure 7.2 A 3-step-answering Template

Repeating the question means to repeat the question, make comments on the question and forecast how the question will be answered. These techniques can be applied alone or together, and can be beneficial to the presenter, the questioner as well as the audience in many aspects. Firstly, it will clarify the question for other audience. For example, if the audience failed to hear or to understand the question clearly, they could still get what it is after the presenter repeat the question. Secondly, the audience could find it easier to follow the answer, if the presenter can tell them how the question is going to be answered at the beginning of the answer. Thirdly, it will help the presenter win some time to think. As has been discussed, one of the problems presenters may have is that they have no time to think about the question before answering. By using "delay" expressions such as commenting on the question and/or repeating the question, the presenter can buy some time to think and organize the answer.

Offering response of the question is the most important part of an answer. It is where the presenter tells what the facts are or explains his or her ideas. If the question or your answer concerns with the point(s) in your presentation, don't forget to show the corresponding PowerPoint slide(s) when you are answering it.

Checking serves as the final step of a direct answer. It is to check if any further explanations or elaborations are needed with the questioner. So, make sure you have offered the information expected. Otherwise, additional questions may be asked.

Tasks

1 Work in groups and summarize the general steps you can follow when answering a question directly. Complete the table below with your discussion result.

Stages of answering	Steps to follow	Skills related	Language expressions
Before answering	Understand the question		
While answering			
	Comment the question		
	Answer the question		
After answering			

UNIT 7 Asking and Answering Academic Questions

❷ Read the short paragraph and prepare 3 normal and easy questions according to the content. Then work with a partner to do the role-play in turns. As a questioner, you need to ask your partner one question at a time. As an answerer, you need to answer the question directly taking the 3-step-answering template.

China's technology giant Huawei leads the list of the country's strategic emerging industry leading companies in 2021, according to a report by the China Business Industry Research Institute. China Mobile and China Telecom grabbed second and third on the list, which focuses on the new generation of information technology, new materials and high-end equipment manufacturing. The list was formed based on companies' annual business income.

(Source: *China Daily* . 2021. China's top 10 emerging industry leaders in 2021. 11-17. From *China Daily* website.)

7.3.3 Avoidance

In many cases, a direct answer should be avoided due to certain reasons, such as limited knowledge, language problems, time limitation, offensive questions, confidential consideration, limitation of authorization, and irrelevant questions.

Some specific skills can be adopted in avoidance. They can be used alone or together according to the specific condition.

1) Direct Avoidance: Apology + Excuse

Direct avoidance means to decline the question, but it's not to say nothing. Instead, an apology and the reasons for the declining are always expected. Meanwhile, make sure you indicate you will check it later and is willing to discuss after the session.

2) Concession: Thanks/Agreement + Transition

To make concession means to show appreciation or agreement of the questioner's ideas to some extent, and then transit with adversative conjunctions like "but" and "however". This way of declining can make it easier for the questioner to accept the answer, and is effective in avoiding conflicts.

3) Delay in Answering

To avoid an immediate answer, the presenter can delay it by assuring the audience that the question will be answered later. One of the ways is to leave the question temporarily and indicate a time after the presentation to answer it. Another common way is to tell the questioner that the answer they expect will not be given for the moment but something else related may be mentioned.

4) Vague Expression

Although conciseness and accuracy are required in academic communication, vague expression is adopted at sometimes when an answer cannot or need not to be definite and clear, or when the information is not appropriate to be revealed in the answer. Hedging expression like "may" "probably" "about" "tend to" "seem" "likely" are usually used to achieve the goal of avoidance.

5) Attention Distracting

Shifting the questioner's attention from the presenter to distractors like another person or thing is also considered as a common technique to avoid direct answers. For example, the presenter can draw the questioner's attention to someone else at present, such as the audience, the chair of the session, other researchers, colleagues, or a written material like a book or a journal paper. However, before shifting the attention, the rationale of doing this should be explained. If not, it will confuse the audience a lot. Meanwhile, to complete the distraction, a new question related to the original question or the distractor will be needed.

Tasks

❶ Discuss in groups on the following questions. Then summarize and complete the table below.

1. For what types of questions an avoidance of answer should be given?
2. Which skills of avoidance should be used for each type of these questions?

Skills of avoidance	Types of question	Example questions	Language expressions
Direct avoidance			
Concession			
Delay in answering			
Vague expression			
Attention distracting			

UNIT 7 Asking and Answering Academic Questions

❷ In small groups, ask each other the following awkward and difficult questions. Or you can ask the example questions you wrote in the table of Task 1. Try to begin answering quickly using the skills of avoidance.

1. What is the population of unmarried adults in Asia?
2. How quickly are global temperatures going to rise?
3. How many words are there in English?

⟩ Language Toolkit

Useful Expressions and Sentence Patterns of Dealing with Questions:

1) Welcome the Question

- I'm very glad that you asked the question.
- I appreciate that you are interested in my presentation.
- I appreciate your question.
- Thank you very much for your question.
- I'd be delighted to answer your question.

2) Euphemism

- I've noticed your saying…I'm sorry to bring this up, but you seem to had a misunderstanding of…
- I'm afraid, you might have made a mistake in…
- I don't like but I have to say…
- I don't think it is appropriate/proper…
- If I'm not mistaken, I understand your question is about…
- I'm sorry to say that the remarks in your question should be regarded as less friendly.

3) Hedging

- can/should/could/would/may/might…
- probably/possibly/approximately/potentially/likely
- seem to/tend to
- about/around/roughly/nearly/almost…
- It seems that…
- It is likely/probable/possible that…

4) Ask the Questioner to Repeat

- Pardon?/Beg your pardon. /I beg your pardon.
- What was that?/What was the last word, please?
- Sorry?
- Sorry, I didn't hear/catch/follow/understand/get what you've said. Would you please say it again?/Could you repeat it, please?
- Would you mind repeating the question?

5) Check Your Comprehension of the Question

- Sorry, I'm not quite sure of your question. Could I understand it like…?
- I am sorry. I am not quite sure what your question is.
- I'm afraid I don't quite understand what you are getting at.
- I don't see what you mean.
- If I understood your question correctly, you want to know…
- …I guess that's what you're asking me, right?
- Are you asking me a question about…?
- Are you referring to…?
- To the best of my knowledge, you were asking me about…Am I right?
- It seems to me that what I have been asked perhaps means…Was that your question?

6) Delaying Expressions

- Filler words: um, err, yeah, well, OK, alright, right…
- Let me see…
- I suppose I'd say…
- How can I put it?…

7) Positive Comments

- That's a(n) good/interesting/enlightening/excellent/challenging/key question.
- I think you've put forward a very good question.
- I think you hit the nail on the head.
- I think this question has some insight.

8) Citation of the Presentation Content

- As I have mentioned/discussed/introduced/reported/proposed/suggested/concluded…in (which section & which point, e.g. the end of the Section One) of my presentation...

- Concerning this point, I think I have touched on it in my speech...
- To answer your question, I will just repeat what I said in my talk...
- Let's turn back to...of my presentation.
- I'd like to repeat...of what I said just now.
- Please look at this picture/graph/slide. I think it will help you understand...

9) Deal with Questions One at a Time

- That's really two/three/...different questions. Let me deal with them one at a time.
- Your first question/point was about...The second question was about ...The last question was about...
- I'll deal with your second question first, if I may.

10) Answer Questions Partially

- Since time is limited, I would like to answer the first/last/...point of your question.
- For the time being, I would like to answer your question of...
- One of the questions you put forward is about...
- All right, I'll now say a few words about...And I think that might be the answer to your last question.

11) Check the Questioner's Satisfaction

- Did I answer your question?
- This is my answer. Is it enough for your question?
- I hope it makes sense to you.
- I don't know if this is a satisfactory answer.
- I think this might be the answer to your question.
- Did your question get answered?

12) Answering Directly

- As far as I am concerned...
- According to my understanding...
- As I learnt it, ...
- In my opinion, ...
- Personally, ...

- I think/believe/assume …

- Let me try to answer the question from a general perspective/two aspects…

Useful Sentence Patterns of Avoiding an Answer:

1) Direct Avoidance

- Sorry, I am afraid I know very little about the matter.

- I am very sorry, but I'm afraid it is more than I can do to answer your question at the moment.

- Since the time is very short, I would like to answer your question after this speech session, if you don't mind. Is that alright?

- Personally, I think that is quite another thing.

- I'm afraid I know little about the question you asked. I will have to consult about it with …Sorry.

- This is an extremely difficult question to answer. If you don't mind, I'd like to discuss it with you at length on another occasion.

- I haven't had time to look into that, sorry.

2) Concession

- I see your point, but…

- I think what you said also sounds reasonable, but…

- I am very glad that you are interested in…However, …

- I agree with you on…, but…

3) Delaying the Answer

- I think you have raised a very interesting question, but it cannot be answered in a few words. In order to give the audience a comprehensive and also specific answer, please allow me to make appropriate preparation and give you the answer next time.

- Thank you very much for your enlightening remarks on…And according to your suggestion, I would like to make some preparations on the topic of…If it is not too much trouble, may we meet at…this evening/after the session so that I could have another chance of giving you a further account on the subject?

- For the time being, I would like to answer your questions after the session, if you don't mind.

- Thank you for your interest in my point of view. If it's convenient with you, I hope we

UNIT 7 Asking and Answering Academic Questions

can meet…so that I can give you a detailed answer to your question.
- I'll come back to that in a minute, if that's all right. I'd need to think about that.
- That's an important question, but it's really too complex to deal with now. Would you mind that we have a private discussion on it after the session?

4) Vague Expression

- …is about/around something between…and…
- I will certain…at an appropriate time.
- Well, it seems to indicate that…tend to…
- I suppose that…probably/possibly…

5) Attention Distraction

- I think it would be better if it is answered by Professor…than by me.
- Professor…would be a better person to answer your question since he has done a lot of work in this field.
- Fortunately, Professor…, who is an authority in this area, is here. I think no one is more suitable than him to answer your question.
- Perhaps my colleague Dr.… here has some better ideas.
- I think it would be better if Professor… were to make some comments on this matter.
- Mr.… and I work in the same laboratory, so I would leave that question to Mr.… I am sure that Mr.… will certainly give you a satisfactory answer.
- I am very interested in your question. Therefore, I would like to know how you…
- Our result of the experiment indicates that the direct method is in good agreement with …By the way, what about your experimental results?
- The design is generally based on the calculation of Professor…Professor…once said that…He also said…
- If you are interested in…, I suggest you take a look at…of my book/paper entitled…

> Reflection & Practice

1. Which skills do you think are most helpful in dealing with questions?
2. What other possible suggestions do you have on dealing with questions?
3. Can you summarize some particular etiquette that we should follow when answering questions?
4. Work in a group of 4 to 5 members.

1) Prepare a short individual presentation on your research direction.

2) Take turns to be the presenter and the questioner:

As a presenter, you should:

- deliver your presentation in the group;
- invite questions from other group members after the presentation;
- answer the questions in the proper and polite manner using the skills and techniques you learnt in this unit;

As a questioner, you should:

- listen attentively to others' presentations;
- ask related questions adopting the template, skills and etiquette you learnt in this unit.

3) Write feedback on others' performance in dealing with questions and exchange your feedback.

Unit 8
Corresponding for Academic Purposes

 Learning Objectives

- To identify the purposes and language features of academic emails;

- To be familiar with the structure and main details of the major types of emails;

- To reply emails with more effective techniques to achieve success in academic correspondence;

- To be familiar with the media platforms for international academic exchange.

Pre-learning Questions

1. Have you ever written English emails for academic communication purposes?
2. Why is it important to write an appropriate academic English emails?
3. How can you accomplish your communicative purpose via English emails?

In this unit, you will learn how to achieve your communication purposes in academic correspondence. Purposes and language features of academic emails will be introduced. You will practise the strategies to present your academic experience and achievements in practical ways to apply for joint training program and cooperation projects, to apply for an overseas study opportunity and answer the reviews from the journal reviewers, and so forth. You will also get to know how to communicate effectively with foreign scholars within the framework of the basic norms of intercultural academic communication with national confidence and cultural confidence.

8.1 Introduction of Academic Correspondence

Classroom Voice

Richard finds it an academic routine to write and answer emails to exchange thoughts, to report progress or to make applications, etc. Though Richard is sure that academic correspondence is different from other kind of correspondence since it has its distinctive communication purposes and structures, he expects to know more about academic correspondence writing strategies.

Instructor's Voice

Since it is obvious that academic correspondence is an indispensable part of one's academic communication, it's essential to have an overall view of English academic correspondence and understand the types, various purposes and characteristics of it.

8.1.1 Definition of Academic Correspondence

Academic correspondence is the usual communication media between students and professors, editors, academic peers or school academic management staff. Though career-starting or experienced researchers may do it in other ways than via writing emails, like making phone calls, sending telegraphs or posting paper letters or cards, emails are now a prevailing way for researchers to correspond for a variety of academic purposes. Thus, this unit will mainly discuss about emails as an academic correspondence means.

8.1.2 Various Purposes of English Academic Correspondence

Academic correspondence, either within a circle or outside of an organization, usually has a specific purpose or more, reporting laboratory progress, requesting information, describing a solution to a technical problem, expressing an academic interest, networking, and so forth. A good academic email writer may have his/her own writing style or personality shown in the lines though, being explicit about the purpose(s) of the writing in a polite and clear way is widely accepted and encouraged. Although the academic purposes may vary, there are some common ones as follows:

1) Letter of Application

(1) To make an application for overseas study or academic visit/exchange: There are several compulsive components for an overseas study or visit application: Curriculum Vitae, personal statement, a research proposal.

(2) To express expectation of joining in an overseas academic team or a project: Researchers usually apply for the participation in a foreign university based program or project with support academically or financially.

2) Cover Letter

To submit research papers for international conference presentation or possible publication in international journals with a brief letter which mainly highlights research innovations involved.

3) Invitation Letter

To invite foreign scholars and experts to participate in academic events in China.

4) Inquiry Letter

To inquire about some information or details concerning international academic conferences or other academic exchange activities.

5) Reply Letter

(1) Letter of response to review: To respond to the received letters about review comments.

(2) Letter of acceptance: To give an acceptance reply to the received invitation letter.

(3) **Letter of declination:** To decline the received invitation letter with strong reasons and best wishes.

6) Letter of Thanks or Apology: To establish or maintain an academically social relationship.

> **Tasks**

Identify and write down the purposes of the following emails.

Material 1

Dear Prof. Newman,

I'm a first year PhD candidate from China University of Mining and Technology, Xuzhou, P. R. China, which is one of "211 Project" universities. After I read a lot of papers of my research area, I understand that you are working on community detection and published quite a lot of high level scientific papers. I find your area fits me well, so I write to you to see if you can give me a chance to study in your school. I have been published one paper in the Chinese Core Journal. My CV and published papers have been attached.

And I'm supported by a Chinese National Fund. And this program is a short time (6-24 months) co-education experiences more like a visit scholar program. Students need to acquire an official invitation letter from the prospective tutor/University. Therefore, all I need is an official invitation letter from you. The date of enrollment I'm considering is March 2020. In order to make sure I can catch up with the next year's program, I have to prepare all the application stuff (including your official invitation letter) before December 2019.

I really hope you can respond me as soon as possible. And if you can't make this decision or you have a better recommendation whose research areas fit me well, please inform me.

Yours sincerely,

...

Material 2

Dear Editors and Reviewers,

Thank you for your letter and for the reviewers' comments concerning our manuscript entitled "Semi-supervised Block-wise Architecture Search for Lightweight Generative

Adversarial Network" (Manuscript Number: PR-D-20-00283). Those comments are all valuable and very helpful for revising and improving our paper, as well as the important guiding significance to our researches. We have studied comments carefully and have made revisions carefully. The main revisions in the paper and the responses to the reviewer's comments are as follows.

...

Material 3

Dear Professor Derck Elsworth,

I'm writing to apply for a chance to be a visiting student.

My name is XXX, a PhD student, majoring in mining engineering in China University of Mining and Technology (CUMT), the best mining university in China. My supervisor is Professor XXX, who is a recognized expert in rock mechanics, roadway support and pillar design in China.

This year China Scholarship Council (CSC) provides certain financial assistance (including travel expenses and living expenses) for selected Chinese PhD candidates to take the joint training of a Chinese professor and a foreign counterpart, for periods from 6 to 24 months. I have visited your personal website, and I know that you have extensive research experiences in computational mechanics, mathematical modeling and rock mechanics. I am strongly interested in those and really hope I can join in your research group. Dr. XXX who has studied and worked in your research group, told me that you're an excellent professor both in research and teaching. He recommended me to enter in your research group if possible. Would you give me a chance? I would greatly appreciate it if you can grant me an opportunity for this application.

With the help of my supervisor, I have received a good deal of practical and valuable research training in mining engineering, including rock mechanics and ground control, roadway support, mining methods, etc. Over the years, I have gained experience in research but still need more improvements and have a strong desire to learn something newer and more practical. I am being involved in three research programs from our government and six research projects from coal enterprises, have published five academic papers (refer to my CV). I am familiar with the theory and technology of coal mining and strata control. Not only can I skillfully use the software of UDEC and FLAC3D but also have a good command of English. I'm fully confident that I have the ability to perform well both in my study and research.

Thank you for your attention to my email. My CV, Personal Statement and a brief introduction to CSC Postgraduate Scholarship Program are enclosed. I am looking forward to your reply.

    Best regards.

Sincerely,

XX X

> **Reflection & Practice**

1. Identify the purposes of the selected academic mails or from those letters you have written before.
2. Does your letter serve its purpose? Why or why not?

8.2 Features of English Academic Correspondence

Classroom voice

Richard finds it is not easy at all to write a good email though he has a clear mind of what the letter is written for. Each time he feels confused with the formats and the features of academic emails when he is writing an email, which wastes some of his time and thus causes some barriers to his communication.

Instructor's Voice

When observing the emails, we can see academic emails share the similar elements and formats with most emails. However, academic emails usually require the beautiful use of formal language expressed in an explicit way and a cooperatively polite manner. You will learn them from the sample emails and your writing practice. Discussion on the features will help too.

8.2.1 Formats of Academic Correspondence

1) Main Elements of an Email

- Heading
- Inside address
- Salutation
- Body

- Complimentary close
- Signature

2) Special Elements of an Academic Email
- Subject
- Attachments
- CC (carbon copy)
- BCC (blind-carbon copy)

3) Move Structure of the Main Parts of Academic Emails

(1) Most academic letters have in common the following move structure.
- Greetings
- Statement of the purpose
- Self-introduction
- Qualification for the program/project
- Expectation from the addresser
- Closing with gratitude

4) Content of a Personal Statement

An admission or application essay, also called a personal statement or a statement purpose, written by a prospective applicant, is an essay serving as a common part of the university and college admissions process. Personal statements are often used as a basis for discussion at the admission interview. A personal statement should contain the following contents.

Part One: Elaborate why you are applying for this subject or area, which is the research topic you are interested in, relate the following to the abilities required for your future study;

Related educational background;

Related academic experience and abilities;

Related previous research area and academic achievements.

Part Two: Your understanding of the subject or program;

Your research plan/goals for the current application.

Part Three: How to use the achievements after completion of this program.

Here is an example:

My Personal Statement

In Sep. 2005, I came to the University of..., and began my college life. Admittedly, probably because I just emancipated myself from the stressful, tight and competitive high school life, I had not expended much energy on my professional study when I was a freshman and a sophomore, instead, I participated in many college community organizations, because I thought that it could improve my ability of organization, leadership and comprehensive quality. And I became the chairman of the student union in sophomore year and the head of our college press corps in junior year. Frankly, many aspects of **my ability really improved much** in the process of participating in those activities, but at the same time my grades were not top-notch. So, starting from the third year of my college, I gradually devoted myself to professional learning. And finally, hard work pays off, I **obtained a B.Sc.** and **was awarded as** an "outstanding graduate", which can be received by only the top 5% of graduating seniors. Because of **my excellent performance**, I **got the qualification to pursue my further study** at Department of... without examination and became a postgraduate student on September 1st 2009. From then on, I have strengthened my life direction, hope I could make a progress in the field of mining engineering with my efforts. And at the beginning of Mar. in 2011, I **was recommended** to the Department of Mining Engineering **as one of a few direct PhD candidates of our major**. —Education background

Due to my hard work and rigorous thinking, I **have published five academic paper**s and have completed or have been involved in **three research programs** from our government and **six research projects** from coal enterprises (Details refer to my CV) from Sep. 2009 to now. I have accumulated **rich on-site experience** in the process of doing research and become more perspicacious towards experimental data and phenomenon. **My research capability** has been improved so much that I am very confident to continue scientific research in mining. —**Academic achievements and abilities**

My research areas include roadway support, pillar design, ascending mining in coal seams, process simulation and control. According to the actual situation of China's coal mines and my on-site experience, I find that many problems remain to be solved. For example, what the movement rules of top-coal in full-mechanized caving mining are, how we can improve the recovery rate of thick coal seam better, how to guarantee the stability of roadway with soft surrounding rock or high stress, as well as the realization of coal seams mining reasonable and safe, etc. **Problems above are all those I wish to solve through pursuing my study.** —Research plan or goals

The relative smooth path of my career is not withstanding. **I have always finished my part of every project immaculately. I hope to pursue** more advanced studies and thereby master advanced knowledge and technology **so that I can open more doors and shoulder greater responsibilities. — Why I apply for this program**

Pennsylvania State University is well known for its excellence in Engineering and Science, complete with an accomplished faculty and modern research resources. These should set a good stage for me to exercise my keen mental power and diligence. If I am accepted, I am confident that I can make quick progress in the field of mining engineering. **—Why I apply to your university**

I **plan to return to China after the completion** of my joint training either to teach at the university of...or to lead a high-tech corporation. If I can join in your research group, **I will try my best to study and research, you will find me a good assistant for you**. **—My future plan and commitment to you**

❯ Tasks

❶ Identify the writing purpose and mark the attributes of the following letter.

University of Wollongong

PhD Candidate
School of Mining
China University of Mining and Technology
Xuzhou, Jiangsu Province, 221116

4th January 2019

To whom it may concern

Invitation to the University of Wollongong—XXX

I write to invite XXX born on XXX from China University of Mining & Technology (CUMT), P. R. China, to conduct research work as a visiting scholar at the University of Wollongong, Australia, under the grant of the Chinese Scholarship Council (CSC).

It is anticipated that XXX will be visiting us for a 12 months period in our school under my supervision from September 2010 to September 2011. His research work will be related to the investigation of Mine Fire Prevention and Control Technology in Longwall Goaf Areas and other mine safety issues in underground coal mine environments.

In addition to his academic background, 1 am also satisfied with XXX command of English for his intended PhD studies.

Subject to successfully obtaining his CSC grant, on joining my research group at the University of Wollongong, we will:

- Waive his tuition or bench fees;
- Provide him access to all seminars, classes, and any laboratory facilities that are needed for his intended studies; however he will not be able to take courses for University credit;
- Provide essential supports and funds to cover his research needs.

I look forward to receiving written confirmation of the scholarship so that we can commence the next steps for his study in Australia.

Please feel free to contact me if you need further assistance.

Yours sincerely,

Handwritten Signature

❷ Discuss in groups on the purpose and function of each part of your academic emails and which function is the hardest for your emails to achieve.

Purpose of your email: _____

_____

Have you achieved your purpose? _____

_____

What is the hardest part for you? _____

_____

8.2.2 Language Features of Academic Correspondence

Most academic mails have their distinctive language features different from the daily ones by showing formal and explicit language features.

Read the following sample emails and compare their language features.

1) Well-presented Sample Email

Subject: Help with assignment

Good morning Professor,

I would like to ask for some help with the assignment for class that is due next week. I read the instructions, but I do not understand everything well. Can I meet you to ask some questions? I have time available after our class tomorrow. Is that okay for you? Thank you very much for your time and help.

UNIT 8 Corresponding for Academic Purposes

Sincerely,

Akiko Iwai

2) Poorly Presented Sample Email

Subject: Not clear.

Hey Carina,

this is Juan from your english class, you remember me? i hope u didnt forget your favorite student =)

i have a quesiton, i want to get id card so i can use the city bus.

i think i lost my old one so u know where

i can get the new one?

it will be helpful for me hahaha =)

thank u very much...

Yours,

Juan

(Carlock et al., 2017: 269)

› Tasks

❶ Rewrite the poorly presented sample email in Section 8.2.2 to meet the requirement of formality and explicitness.

❷ Discuss about the language features of the email in Section 8.2.2.

› Reflection & Practice

1. Discuss about the language features, the merits and demerits of the selected academic mails from those you have written.

_____
_____
_____
_____
_____
_____

2. What other distinctive features can you find in the academic correspondence?

8.3 Writing Strategies in Academic Correspondence

Classroom Voice

Anna often fails to express herself satisfactorily in answering the academic emails, so she wants to know if there are some strategies and how she can do it better by applying those effective strategies.

Instructor's Voice

Though no strategies are so effective that they can achieve a quick result in writing a good email, strategies will be introduced and can be observed in the good emails. With a hope to successfully apply for a visiting student in an overseas university, to join in an academic program, or have an article published, let's cultivate the strategies in observing and analyzing the sample writings, and in practising your own emails.

8.3.1 Use You-attitude Rather Than I-attitude

Writers will show politeness and be more considerate when taking a You-attitude in writing an academic email while an I-attitude tends to leave an impression of an impolite and offensive manner. The following reply letter failed to some extent to answer the letter from the professor.

Dear Cao Shan,

I am honored by your interest and would be glad to host you in my research group.

I suggest to apply for a double PhD or for a long period of stay, from 1 to 2 years, to be effective and productive.

Kind regards.

Enrico Zio

UNIT 8 Corresponding for Academic Purposes

Dear Professor Enrico Zio: *— Greetings, purpose and thanks.*

   I am very glad to be invited by you and willing to join in your research group.

   If tuition free is permitted, I <u>decide to</u> apply for a double PhD. <u>Otherwise, I can only apply for stay of 2 years.</u> *— The underlined shows impoliteness*

   I <u>need you to provide me with</u> two documents to qualify for CSC scholarship:

   (1) A formal admission or invitation letter marked the identity as joint PhD. student;

   (2) An English language evidence.

   — Express your gratitude here.

   Best regards.
   Sincerely,

› Tasks

❶ Rewrite the latter sample letter in Section 8.3.1 with an appropriate You-attitude.

Dear Enrico Zio,

_____

_____

_____

_____

_____

❷ Analyze your academic letters and see if you take an appropriate You-attitude manner. Discuss if cultural awareness matters in a You-attitude strategy.

	You-attitude manner
Proof One	
Proof Two	
Proof Three	

8.3.2 More Communicative Strategies in Correspondence

   Here are some communicative strategies for you to bear in your mind when you correspond for an academic communication purpose.

(1) Put a specific and clear subject of your mail rather than a vague one like A question.

(2) Salutations matter. Use appropriate title in the greetings and offer your official name and your academic identity suitable for the relationship between you and the recipient.

(3) Give your documents addicted to the mails a sensible file name to include your name so as to assist the recipient with the file management and the date in the title especially when the document goes through multiple versions. Providing explicit labeling like this also makes it much easier for the recipients to refer to your document.

(4) State the main points and purposes clearly always in a polite and friendly tone even though having to challenge or argue. Negative politeness and reasonable request are more acceptable.

(5) Evaluate the possible relationship, decide the level of formality and use appropriate language.

(6) Show your recipient respect and motivate them to reply.

Tasks

1 Come up with more tips to improve correspondence communication.

More tips: 1. _____
2. _____
3. _____

2 Read the following reviews and response with your focus on the underlined parts. What strategy has been used to achieve the purpose?

Strategies applied: 1. _____
2. _____
3. _____

Title: Anisotropic Characteristics of Coal Fractures and Seepage in the...Mining Area, China
Article Type: Research paper

R1?

Reviewer #1: Visualizing fractures is very important for a naturally fractured rock, particularly for coal, because it will play an important role in coal-bed methane exploration and production. This work quantitatively studied the fracture characteristics using a stereo microscope. It achieves a big progress in fracture visualization of cleats (fractures) in coal. It is innovative, significant and will find applications in natural fracture modeling. I have edited the manuscript and corrected some English issues as attached.

Reviewer #2: The anisotropic characteristics of coal fractures is a hot and important issue in coal reservoir geology, especially taking the CBM exploitation into consideration. Fractures are the main migration pathways for CBM in coals, and their developmental state dominates the permeability of coal reservoirs. The paper gives valuable insights of the coal permeability differences in the parallel and vertical bedding plane directions.

The findings of this paper is useful. However, I have some issues concerning the paper.

(1) Line 46, this sentence is very confusing.

(2) Line 55, the influence of ground stress and reservoir stress on different origin fractures is a very interesting and important aspect. Please add some analysis about this aspect.

(3) Line 87, the anisotropic characteristics of coal fractures is a big scientific question and you declared that geological condition such as coal rank is a very important factor. However, you just focused on coals from the Fukang mining area and the coal ranks in this area change slightly.

In fact, you just analyzed the influence of ground stress and reservoir stress on the fractures, and other factors were ignored. To my mind, your title should be improved to reflect your research more accurately.

(4) The results and discussion part should be narrated separately.

(5) Line 90-94, this paragraph should be merged with the next paragraph. Please add a reference.

(6) Line 255, please add a structure outline map including your sample locations.

(7) Line 258-259, please make sure your finding is universally applicable in all of your samples. How about the contact relations between different macerals?

(8) Line 281-282, you'd better provide a schematic diagram to explain the process.

(9) Line 306-307, you mean exogenous fractures are more intense in your study. If possible, please present the evidence, and label the exogenous and endogenic fractures in your figures.

(10) Line 346, large range. Please give some interpretation. Is this related to the stress direction?

(11) Line 355-356, you declare that "Though later tectonic movement can contribute

to the fractures, natural historical fractures play a dominant role in coal". However, in the following discussion, you just emphasized the influence of ground stress. You did not point out when the natural historical fractures formed. Didn't the inverse-folding effect in the Early Middle Cretaceous play an important role for the formation of the natural historical fractures? Why or why not?

(12) Please add some evaluation of your work to point out the significance of your findings.

I suggest a minor but careful modification.

Reviewer #3:

(1) Line 94: a sampling location is needed here.

(2) The Introduction and Line 99: the part of "2.1. Regional geology and formation conditions" needed to simplify.

(3) Line 120: "national standard" appear two times in ms; Line 224: Fig.3-d showed different thing with the text and should not labeled here, et al., please recheck carefully the full text and revise those mistakes.

(4) Line 122: pictures of sample coal blocks are needed.

(5) Table 1: $R_{o,ave}$ need more explanation.

(6) Line 192: citation needed here.

(7) Line 226: "we found that the fractal dimension of fractures in the parallel direction is smaller than that in the vertical direction", this conclusion which showed in Fig.3-d are not that clear, please reconsider this.

(8) The title of Fig. 4-a, b in text are different samples with the one attached after text. the annotation of Fig. 4 has a mistake.

(9) References need to be updated, especially in introduction and the discussion.

(10) The title is "Anisotropic Characteristics of Coal Fractures and Seepage", but the description of experimental methods, computing method and formula derivation are too much in the text instead of the analysis about anisotropic characteristics of coal fractures and seepage. Please add more discussion about characteristics of coal fractures and seepage.

Reviewer #4: Some statistic methods about fracture porosity, aperture, spacing and permeability have been researched according to the microscope. Following comments should be addressed.

(1) Introduction should be condensed as short as possible.

UNIT 8 Corresponding for Academic Purposes

(2) What's the relationship between the development of coal fractures and tectonic setting or geo-stress?

(3) In Fig.4, the footnotes of parallel and vertical bedding fracture profiles are the same, please revised.

(4) On Page 13, what's the sedimentary tectonic background?

(5) In Part 3.5, only some qualitative description explained, please indicated the quantitative evidences so as to strengthen the ms. This part is the key in the ms.

(6) English language should be edited and checked by native English speaker or English Language Service Co.

R2?

Reviewer #2: Considering the authors have revised carefully and answered the questions raised, I suggest to accept this paper and publish as soon as possible.

Reviewer #3: All the questions which I mentioned in the first review have made a good supplement and revision, so I suggest this manuscript could be published without change this time.

Reviewer #4: Overall, the authors appropriately modified the context according to the reviewers' suggestions. However, overall, this paper needs to be added some explanation to make the results and analysis accurate and reliable. I suggest that this manuscript have Minor revision in the following aspects:

(1) Page1 Line 16. "The fracture aperture, fracture porosity, fracture density and fracture connectivity" can be described as "The aperture, porosity, density and connectivity of coal fractures".

(2) Page 1 Line 27. The authors declare "provides potential theoretical guidance of CBM exploitation". Maybe the numerical simulation is needed.

(3) Page 2 Line 28. Keywords should be singular.

(4) The Conclusions (1), (2) and (3) are presented as only the results. This part needs to be added some explanation to make the results and analysis accurate and reliable. The paper can be further improved by highlighting the scientific impact of the results of this paper.

(5) The left three photomicrograph should be noted as a,b,c and explained the relationship between parallel/vertical bedding fractures in Fig. 7.

(6) In Fig. 9, the authors should explain the detailed exogenous or endogenic fractures,

such as using the arrows, fractures characteristics and labeling the coal composition.

(7) The last page "Fig. 6 The ratio of fracture width…" should be "Fig. 10 The ratio of fracture width…".

(8) Figure captions: Ensure that each illustration has a caption. A caption should comprise a brief title (not on the figure itself) and a description of the illustration. Keep text in the illustrations themselves to a minimum but explain all symbols and abbreviations used.

R3?

Reviewer #4: The secondly revised ms was appropriately modified by the authors. I suggest accepting the ms for the publication in the journal.

❸ Read the response letter and see if the letter responded appropriately.

Dear Editors and Reviewers,

Thank you very much for your letter and for the reviewers' comments concerning our manuscript entitled "Semi-supervised block-wise architecture search for lightweight Generative Adversarial Network" (Manuscript Number: PR-D-20-00283R2). Although there are fewer revision comments than last time, these comments are essential to improve the quality of our papers. We have studied and made revisions carefully. We try our best to explain some of the doubts raised by the experts. The revisions in the paper and the responses to the reviewers' comments are as the following:

Reviewer #1:

Reviewer #1: Thanks for the authors' efforts in revising the manuscript. In this revision, my concerns are addressed by reorganizing the structure of the method part and updating the comparison with recent research. It can be accepted if other reviewers have no further questions.

Our response: Thank you very much for your recognition of our work. We will try to make up for the shortcomings of current research and put more energy on improving network efficiency.

Reviewer #2:

Your corrections and the addition of new material was really successful regarding the comments of both mine and the rest reviewer. Although it is now more clear your overall proposal, I still have some considerations about your total presentation.

UNIT 8 Corresponding for Academic Purposes

(1) In Table 1, please make some more formal modifications: do, ? do: or just do—B1. B2, ... → please fill with an arbitrary parameter, g = G(I'), ? remove comma.

(2) I was really confused with the results in Figure 5, if the color identification depicts the proportion of the labeled data, then the error rate should decrease, since we have the actual label of these instances. But your present the opposite behavior. Please clarify.

(3) Figures 6 and 7: please provide x-axis and y-axis title.

(4) In Table 5 you mention the Mean Teacher as a fully supervised method, however this is a semi-supervised one. Could you mention how this acted under such a scenario?

I believe also that you have to share your code, to further facilitate the reader about your implementation. Moreover, which was the most beneficial scenario for boosting the performance of your model regarding the SSL stage? It is not clear which labeled ratio is efficient for training your initial model before the block structure is adopted.

Our response: Thank you very much for your encouragement and suggestions, which are very helpful to improve our paper.

(1) We have modified the 'do' 'B1, B2' and 'g=G(I'),'.

Table 8.1 The Pipeline of the Propoeed Semni-GNAs

Step	Implementation
1	Input the original I, perform random occlusion, and output I_1
1	While t <max_ epoch do:
2	Set basic blocks structure, $B_1(i)$, $B_2(i)$...,
2	Build generator structure based on block,
2	$g = G(I')$
3	$d = D(g(I'), x)$
4	$t = t + 1$
5	Record and compare the accuracy.
6	Restructure the neural architecture and repeat the training process.
7	After several rounds of architecture searches, the optimal structure
7	(S) and best results are chosen and executed on the mobile device.

(2) Thank you for your comments. Considering that our analysis of Figure 5 is not comprehensive enough, we have made corresponding additions and modifications.

Analyzing the experimental results of different proportions under the same number of training steps, it can be concluded that in the early stage, the smaller the proportion of the influence of the true labels on the overall loss, the better performance can be temporarily achieved. However, in the middle and late stages, the higher the proportion of real labels, the faster the error rate decreases. When the number of training steps reaches 20,000, the gray error rate is the lowest. This proves that increasing the number of training steps can improve the performance of the model. From another perspective, the proposed semi-supervised method can obtain satisfactory results in a shorter training time. We believe that this result is related to the game principle of GAN. However, considering that we have a built-in classifier in the discriminator to predict image category and image authenticity. The experimental results are affected by real labels, pseudo labels and generated images, so it is necessary to control the ratio of real labels. In this case, we recommend using 50% of real labels in the experiment to get more convincing experimental results faster.

(3) Thank you for your reminder, we have added x and y axis titles to Figure 6 and Figure 7.

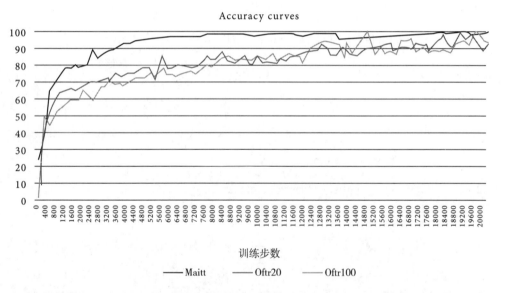

(4) Thank you very much for your reminder. We have not stated clearly here. The Mean-Teacher in Table 4 is indeed a semi-supervised method, but what we compare in Table 5 is its fully-supervised experimental results. We have already made supplements accordingly.

It should be noted that Mean-Teacher's fully-supervised experimental result is shown in Table 4, and its semi-supervised result is shown in Table 5.

UNIT 8 Corresponding for Academic Purposes

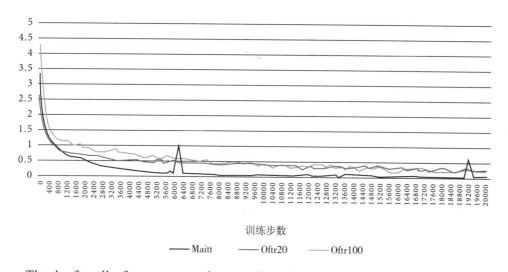

Thanks for all of your suggestions, and we have uploaded a set of baseline code. The purpose of our work is to achieve both image generation and classification in a semi-supervised learning method, and to make the model lightweight and efficient enough to be quickly implemented on small mobile devices, and many parameters are required to work together. In this case, we should not only consider classification performance, so as mentioned in the analysis of Figure 5, we recommend using 50% of real labels in the experiment. From our point of view, although theoretically the more labels, the better the experimental results should be. In fact, even in fully supervised learning, there are many poorly performing networks. Many studies have proved that when the model is well designed, whether it is semi-supervised, weakly supervised or unsupervised, it can perform well. At present, a weaklier-supervised learning method has been proposed which only uses one image-level label for a category, and has achieved good results. Therefore, we believe that the influence of the label on the model's performance is not decisive. As mentioned above, our model is based on GANs. In our method, the discriminative classifier is affected by real images, real labels, generated images and pseudo labels. Due to the game principle of GANs, it is different from ordinary CNN network. We are loyal to the real experimental results and show them. We believe that the overall trend is positive, thus proving the effectiveness of our approach. We are so sorry that we cannot give an in-depth explanation of the "black box" of neural networks from the perspective of interpretable neural networks, which is beyond our current research field. But this is indeed a promising research direction, and there are also members in our team who are working on this. We will explore the principles of neural networks more in future research to make our work more comprehensive.

Thanks again to the editors and experts for their valuable comments and suggestions. We have tried our best to improve this paper. If there are other problems with the paper, please let us know.

Best wishes,

Zhang ××, Wang ××, Gao ××

Language Toolkit

Useful Sentence Patterns of English Correspondence:

- I am writing to you to apply for...
- Thank you for your reminder.
- Thanks for your encouragement and suggestion.
- If there are..., please let us know.
- It can be accepted if...
- Considering that our analysis of...is not comprehensive enough, we have made corresponding additions and modifications.
- All the questions which I mentioned in the first review have made a good supplement and revision.

Reflection & Practice

1. Write an academic email to the class email box or QQ group. It will be commented on within your group.
2. Illustrate the structure and main details of one type of mails with a written outline. Retell one of your mails with convincing techniques.
3. In the era of "We Media", introduce some such media platforms for international academic exchange, especially those used in your fields.

Part Four

Advanced Academic English Communication

Unit 9
Identifying International Conference Information

Learning Objectives

- To perceive the possible rewards of attending international academic conferences;

- To know how to seek the information about the upcoming conferences;

- To understand the major types of academic conferences;

- To identify and understand the key elements of call for papers or conference notices;

- To learn about the most prestigious conferences in your research field and determine the academic conference you aim to attend;

- To acquire information about the leading scientists in your field and draw inspiration from their experiences.

Pre-learning Questions

1. What will you as a graduate student gain when you attend academic conferences?
2. Do you know the major types of international academic conferences and where to find the related information?
3. What are the principal activities of an international academic conference?
4. What key messages are conveyed in a call for papers or conference notice?
5. What are the pioneering academic conferences in your research field? And what is the international academic conference you aim to participate?
6. Who are the keynote speakers in your research field? Search online for their past experiences and see what inspiration you can obtain from them.

In this unit, you are going to learn about how to make preparations for attending international academic conferences. You will first of all look at the necessity of communicating with researchers in professional meetings and see how these valuable experiences will facilitate your academic and future career development. And then you will learn how to retrieve the information about forthcoming academic events via various channels and how to sort out the principal details, for example, the various kinds of meetings, the major conference activities as well as the paper submission information. All of the careful planning and deliberate preparations will pave the way for a fruitful conference attending experience.

9.1 Benefits of Attending International Academic Conferences

Classroom Voice

Sam, a freshman graduate student, feels somehow confused about why his mentor urges him to attend international academic conferences. Although he seems to realize experiences of this kind will be rewarding to his research and future career, but is not quite certain about the possible benefits if he participates in an academic conference.

Instructor's Voice

Conferences, whose Latin root, "fer", means to bring or carry, refer to the large-scale meetings which are focused on one particular subject or bring people together with the same interest.

In today's ever-changing world, attending academic meetings has been a "must" to survive in academia. Many researchers have become aware of this fact and the number of conferences and attendees increases dramatically. The following part elaborates on what a graduate student will possibly profit from the participation in addition to sightseeing.

Academic conferences are an important activity for a young scholar which entails tremendous significance for his or her career development.

- One of the major reasons why one should attend a conference is that academic conferences will update a researcher on the newest findings in an academic discipline. A research article published in a professional journal has often been redrafted many times, with several months passing between the first draft being submitted and the date of publication. However, most academic conferences accept the latest findings, so participating in these events is a valuable way to keep up with the recent advances in a field. The participants have opportunity to communicate with academics and experts from all over the world on the emerging technological breakthroughs. Their horizon can be consequently broadened and their research work can hopefully be upgraded accordingly.

- Presenting papers is also one of the main objectives for conference participants. The presenters share their ideas in front of experts and colleagues of the similar fields of study and invite questions. The positive feedback and constructive criticism about the research will ultimately strengthen the work.

- The attendees obtain the most value from following up with everyone whose presentation caught their attention. This could be realized by approaching the speaker in the hall or attending conference social events that can sometimes be as beneficial as showing up at technical sessions. It is always useful to hear others' opinions on careers and research, especially when the relaxed conversation takes place over a coffee or a beer. Therefore, mealtimes are a great chance to talk about work or discuss the presentations with the most impact. Many conference organizers also hold activities targeted at young researchers, and they are a really helpful way to develop new contacts.

- The exchange of ideas on fields of interest paves the way for potential collaboration and joint research projects. Networking, like in any other professional field, is very important in academia. Socializing with the colleagues and friends at coffee breaks, lunches and other social activities may open doors to being invited to join collective research projects. It could be edited books, special issues in peer-reviewed journals or funding application.

- Networking plays a fundamental role in getting a job in academia. In most cases, the job selection procedure is fair and transparent. But ultimately, with a similar CV, selection committee members are most likely to choose someone that they know and get along with. Although research work is mostly individual in nature, it has a social side to it.

- Any attendees who take part in academic conferences aim for publication. Some selected papers can be published and indexed while all accepted abstracts are published in the conference proceedings.

- Last but not least, an international conference helps establish the attendee's scientific reputation. One can not only meet the renowned respectable professors from every corner of the world but also communicate with many promising young researchers as well. The conference serves as an invaluable occasion to build up and promote the participant's profile among the researchers of the similar interests.

› Tasks

1 Discuss in a small group of 3 to 4 persons. Can you think of any other benefits of attending international conferences like improving your English? Elaborate on each point.

2 Share with your group members your past conference experiences. How many academic meetings have you attended like graduation defenses or seminars? How did you feel each time, confident or nervous? What have you gained from those experiences?

› Language Toolkit

Useful Expressions and Sentence Patterns of Talking About the Significance of Attending International Conferences:

- to expose one's ideas to experts in your field
- to have the opportunity to meet new people
- to build strong professional relationships

- to make a revision of my paper/thesis
- to deepen my understanding of…
- to build up my profile/reputation as a young researcher
- to forge a network/relationship with…
- the dressing codes
- to break the ice
- It is rewarding to do sth.
- It is beneficial/good for sb. to do sth.
- …benefits me a lot in that…
- An academic conference is a great way to…
- It is vital/important/fundamental to do sth.
- …provides me with invaluable chance to…
- …plays an (increasingly) important role in…
- This is an opportunity for me to…
- For students and researchers, academic conferences help to…
- …is one of the main objectives of an academic conference participant.

> Reflection & Practice

Read the following article and see whether you agree or disagree upon the following 5 points. Try to see if you have any other suggestions regarding how to network effectively at an academic conference.

Top Five Ways to Better Academic Networking (Excerpt)

1) Talk about the papers. At the first conference I attended I was surprised by what a mess I was at the morning tea table. While everyone else seemed to know people and slip into little chatty groups, I stood there holding my cup feeling as awkward as a teenager at a blue light disco. This was disconcerting because I am normally at ease socially (My mother worked hard on this. Believe me—I am not a natural).

When I got home I told one of my supervisors how I felt and he gave me some advice for starting up conversation, one of which was "just talk about the papers". So now, if I am lonely, I look for another solo player and introduce myself. Then I ask about which is the best paper they have seen so far. After this the conversation usually starts to flow.

2) Become social glue. Point two follows on from point one. Once you have made a friend by bonding over papers it is easy to slip into just hanging out with them at the next break, but it's important to resist the temptation. However it is rude to just ignore your new buddy—the point is to make lasting friends remember? So I usually suggest to my new friend that we try to befriend another solo player together. I then try to build from there, periodically leaving my new group to bring in new people.

The first day can be hard work, but it pays off. If you persevere, by the second day you will have met at least four or five people and have been asked out to dinner—I guarantee it. If you go to repeat conferences this is a strategy which pays greatly over time.

3) Be prepared. Along with the obvious things you need, such as business cards, computer and phone chargers etc, don't forget to take extra headache medicine! Lots of people at conferences are a little stressed out/jet-lagged/hung over and many of them forget to be prepared for this.

Luckily I am a bit of a fan of the old headache medication and consequently have made lifelong friends after producing magic pills from my bag. The power of bathroom bonding—where such requests are usually aired—cannot be overlooked and provides another avenue to activate the strategy outlined in points one and two.

4) Remember the rule of four (or less). There will be times, of course, when you want to talk to some established "big names". They are usually surrounded by hangers-on and people they met when they were newbies at conferences and have known for years, so this can be difficult.

Since I am not a natural, I always think about these social problems analytically. This is why, some time ago, I read with interest "Grooming, gossip and the evolution of language" by Robin Dunbar. One of Dunbar's more fascinating theories is that our brains can only handle so many people talking at once. In fact he claims our capacity is limited to four.

In groups greater than four, one person will be "holding the floor", for instance by telling some kind of story, or the group will split. The next time you are at a party test out this theory by trying to join a group of four and see what happens (and let me know the result!).

When your target "star" is talking in a pair it can seem rude to break in, but you can do it if you hover near them and try to make eye contact. If there is a group of three however it is much easier and you should go for it by just joining in and saying something—humans love a fourth.

However if the star is already in a group of four, remember if you make the attempt now you will have to be a "group breaker"—or a listener. Being a group breaker has a social cost—it's likely you will need to work harder to not appear rude.

Make sure you have some good questions prepared for the star so you can sustain the conversation after all this effort!

5) Don't drink alcohol—especially at conference dinners. I know that one of my good friends (who shall remain nameless) would violently disagree with me on this point. He talks fondly of the friendships he has forged over a red wine or five at conferences. However, unlike my friend, who is kind and funny under the influence, I do not hold my liquor well.

They say your true self comes out when you are drunk and I turn into a clumsy, affectionate and compulsive over sharer. I do not come across as a smart and switched on person who can talk the finer points of Actor Network Theory on demand—which is how I would rather be remembered. I have had to work hard at being relaxed without needing a drink around my peers and colleagues, but it has been worth it.

9.2 Information Sources on International Academic Conferences

Classroom Voice

Knowing that participating in academic conferences is a golden opportunity for a young researcher, Sam intends to attend one of them. However, there seems to be an overwhelming amount of information on the Internet. Where can Sam find reliable and updated sources of academic conferences?

Instructor's Voice

If it is your first time to attend a research conference, finding the right event to attend is no piece of cake. With over 200,000 academic conferences all over the world, it is vital to fully understand how to select one that matches your academic goals. In the following part, some useful ways to retrieve conference information will be introduced.

There are various ways to find the related academic conferences according to a specific research area or topic, among which the Internet is definitely the most convenient means. The following lists some of the most trusted websites to find the upcoming international conferences. These conference databases offer a convenient way to narrow down the great number of academic events out there. Tick boxes and filters and the user can search for conferences with "Call for Papers" (CFP) or conference notices. The search can be done by location, subject or keyword terms.

- http://conf.cnki.net: a collection of academic conferences covering various disciplines

- both in China and abroad.
- http://meeting.sciencenet.cn: mostly academic conferences held in China, covering engineering science, life science, mathematical science, medical sciences, chemical science, and management science, etc.
- http://www.allconferences.com: a global conference directory of over 100,000 conferences, conventions, trade shows, exhibits, expos and seminars.
- https://www.elsevier.com/en-gb/events/conferences: academic events organized by Elsevier in agricultural and biological sciences, computer science, engineer, environmental science, medicine, chemistry, physics, etc.
- https://www.conference-service.com/conferences: a web-based conference management system offering conference information on mathematics, engineering, physics, chemistry, informatics, earth studies, life sciences, education, history & philosophy of science & technology, etc.
- https://www.ieee.org/conferences/index.html: a search engine operated by the world's largest professional organization which helps to seek meetings on electronic and electrical engineering, computer science, agriculture, medicine, biology, etc.

In addition to the online conference databases, social media provides a personalized channel to disseminate information. Friends and colleagues who have spotted a Call For Papers (CFP) will recommend it to others. With WeChat, the subscribers can expand a personal recommendation to a wider circle of peer academicians. "Following" people in the same research field and searching for the meetings they organize or attend is an effective way to find events. But the information seeker should be careful to separate meaningful recommendations from automated plugs. Like the online conference databases, there is an over-abundance of information on WeChat.

The influential academic activities are usually hosted by large organizations. Following these institutions or organizations via membership, or social media provides a great way to keep in touch in regard to conferences. These large events attract a large number of researchers, have world-leading experts and tend to have a greater catering budget. Meanwhile, academic conferences at this level can be competitive to present at and so the applications for these are more likely to result in rejection. Try not to be disheartened though, because sometimes they also result in success with an excellent chance to disseminate the ideas.

It is equally advisable to visit the notice board or informational wall of the organization for information on upcoming academic conferences. The printed CFPs are often posted there to catch the attention of potential attendees.

UNIT 9 Identifying International Conference Information

Last but not least, professors and academicians of the academic societies usually get invitations for upcoming conferences from various organizations, so contacting them also helps retrieve the relevant conference information.

> **Tasks**

❶ How did you learn about the upcoming academic activities in the past? What are the new sources you have learned in this section?

❷ Are there any other reliable information sources for academic conferences? Please share them in class.

> **Reflection & Practice**

Try one or two of the sources that you have never used before and search for at least two international academic meetings in your specific research field. Share your findings in a small group of 3 or 4 people.

9.3 Varieties of Academic Conferences

There are various types of academic events. Among them, seminars, workshops, conferences, conventions and symposiums are meetings that are held mostly in academic environments. Many people remain confused and cannot tell one from another because of their similarities and overlapping in the way they are arranged and attended. However, there are differences pertaining to the number of delegates, topics covered, duration, which will be discussed in the following part.

1) Conferences

Conferences tend to be the largest in scale compared with other types of academic events. They can number anywhere between dozens to thousands of attendees who can be industry or government researchers, sometimes administrators. They usually have a general topic or several more specific topics and last for a few days.

Conferences tend to be the most prestigious forms of events as well, and therefore they are the place where the researchers most desire the opportunity to present their work as a speech or a poster. Participants submit abstracts to present their findings (oral or poster), capture the attention of colleagues, get feedback, refine presentation skills, learn from others in the field and network. In addition, conferences usually include a number of presentations by prominent speakers in addition to poster sessions in which researchers present their ideas and discoveries in a visual format.

2) Conventions

A convention is often an annual or biannual event that brings people of a shared interest to learn advancements in the particular field and make networking connections. These events are often recurring, and are usually scheduled at a specific time each year. Conventions, like conferences, tend to have keynote speakers, presentations that familiarize attendees with trends within the particular research field as well. The organizers usually are academic societies or professional associations.

3) Symposiums

A symposium is a formal meeting in an academic setting where participants are experts in their fields. The experts present or deliver their opinions or viewpoints on a chosen topic for discussion. Symposia are particularly good for student speakers as it allows them to practise and get feedback on their own work.

It would be right to label a symposium as a small scale conference as the number of delegates is smaller. There are the usual discussions on the chosen topic after the experts have presented their speeches. One of the prominent characteristics of a symposium is that it covers a single topic or subject and usually all the lectures given by experts are completed in a single day.

4) Seminars

Seminars are typically lecture-oriented meetings with a comparatively smaller group of people—from five to over a hundred. They are mostly held at a classroom environment, and audio visual aids are an indispensible part of the presentation in a seminar. Seminars are often presented by one or several chief speakers on a specific topic who tend to impart the latest knowledge and new trends in the field of research. The participants, who share a common interest in expanding their understanding of a specific topic, listen and then join in the follow-up discussion. They respond to each other and try to make the conversation as helpful, intelligent and inclusive as possible.

Seminars are a valuable place to test out some new ideas or theories that the presenters have been thinking about but are not totally confident with yet. If they are working on a concept or an idea for an experiment but want to hear some feedback on it before developing it further, it is a great way to present it at a seminar. This kind of occasions is perfect for getting honest feedback and suggestions for improvements.

5) Workshops

Workshops are often educational programs designed to teach or introduce practical skills or ideas that can be applied to the attendees' work or daily lives. They are usually interactive training or discussion where participants actively engage in activities rather than passively listen to a lecturer. Workshops are usually moderated by a lecturer or facilitator who shares his or her knowledge or experience about the subject. And the number of participants is purposefully kept relatively low—in many cases less than 25—in order to guarantee individual attention to the participants.

Workshops tend to have a specific, action-oriented purpose featured with an intensive discussion on the subject or particular skill in an academic discipline. They are designed for people who work together or work in the same field and serve as an ideal opportunity to learn new skills and to become familiar with a new topic.

6) Forums

A forum refers to a formally arranged meeting in which people can talk about and discuss a problem or matter, especially of public interest. The attendees come not only from the academia but also from other backgrounds like the industry, government, etc.

7) Web-conferencing

Web conferencing is a term that covers different types of online collaborative services including webinars (在线研讨会), webcasts (网络直播), and web meetings. Using IP or TCP connections over the Internet has paved the way for it. Today various types of web conferencing tools or online meeting tools like VooV Meeting, Blizz, TeamViewer, Zoom or AnyMeeting are used for exchanging views, documents, images and videos between many people at different locations. The users are therefore allowed to perform real-time tasks, for example, sharing the files, modifying the documents as well as discussing the viewpoints.

〉Tasks

❶ Make comparisons between seminars and workshops, conferences and symposiums.

	Conferences	Symposiums
Number of participants		
Theme of the meeting		

(Cont.)

	Conferences	Symposiums
Identity of the participants		
Major activities of the meeting		
Duration		
Number of participants		
Theme of the meeting		
Identity of the participants		
Major activities of the meeting		

❷ Make a short speech on the similarities and distinctions between conferences and symposiums, or seminars and workshops. Deliver it in a small group of not more than 5 students.

❸ Recall your experiences of attending professional meetings. What type of meetings were they, conferences, seminars or symposiums? Try to describe them to your group.

❯ Language Toolkit

Useful Expressions of Discussing International Conference Types and Topics:

- conference
- convention
- symposium
- seminar
- workshop
- forum
- web-conferencing
- background of participants (university/industry researchers; administrators…)
- identity of the attendees (university/industry/government researchers, government

officials…)
- major activities of the meeting (presentations; discussion; training…)
- forms of communication: one-to-many, one-to-one, question and answer session
- chances of in-depth communication with the speakers and other attendees
- passive listeners/active participants
- interaction between the speakers and audience
- to share the latest knowledge and new trends
- to impart hand-on skills
- **Comparison:** likewise, similarly, in the same way, in the same manner
- A is similar to B in…
- A resembles B in…
- A and B share the same feature/characteristic that…
- A bears resemblance to B regarding…
- **Contrast:** by contrast, on the contrary, while, whereas, yet, in contrast, unlike, on the other hand, instead, conversely, nonetheless
- A and B differ in…
- A differs from B in terms of...
- The difference between A and B is/lies in/exists in…
- On the one hand…, but on the other hand…

〉 Reflection & Practice

1. Search for at least two different types of academic meetings in your own research field. Try to compare them in terms of scale, topics, agenda and identity of the attendees. Share your findings in class.

2. The international health crisis about COVID-19 has a major impact on the way academic conferences are held. A large number of conferences have therefore been cancelled or held online. There are certainly distinctions between physical and digital conferences. Discuss in small groups of 3 to 4 persons and discover the major advantages and disadvantages of web-conferencing compared with the face-to-face events.

9.4 Conference Information and Major Conference Activities

Classroom Voice

Stella, a graduate student, has made up her mind to attend an international academic conference. She surfed the Internet and learned about some academic events that attract her attention and interest. Unfortunately, she does not have a clear idea of what will happen during the meetings. She referred to some calls for papers and conference notices, but found some details confusing, like "parallel sessions" and "panel sessions".

Instructor's Voice

The preparation process for participating in international academic conferences could be intimidating for anyone who is new to the industry. However, a thorough understanding of the information concerned including the conference notice and the call for papers is the key to facilitating your work. It serves as the guidelines telling you what the focus of the event is, how you should submit your material properly and what will happen during the conference. These details are elaborated in files like conference notices, call for papers, conference brochures and proceedings.

Published by the conference organizers, the conference notice serves as an advertisement which gives a detailed account of the comprehensive information about the upcoming event, including the name, date, venue, themes, accommodations, participants and paper submission details.

A call for papers (CFP) is an announcement distributed by academic organizations for inviting papers or abstracts from professional researchers to publish or present original and scholarly discoveries in academic journals or conferences. Conference organizers distribute conference call for papers to remind academic communities, elaborating on the broad theme, specific topics to be discussed, time and venue of the conference as well as formalities, for example, what kind of abstract has to be submitted to whom and a deadline.

In addition, a conference brochure provides a list of activities that needs to be followed in the conference. It shows the attendees the major presentations and discussions, their order and the time allocated for each of them. As a first-time conference goer, you need to figure out the meaning of the major conference activities so as to follow the agenda and make your plan.

Last but not least, a conference proceeding is the published record of a conference, congress, symposium, or other meeting, which usually but not necessarily includes abstracts or papers presented by the participants.

The classified conference information necessary for a participant is listed below.

9.4.1 Conference Information

1) General Information

(1) Name

The name of a conference refers to the formal one of the meeting. But abbreviations are often adopted in files like conference notices. For example, The Fourth International Conference on Physics, Mathematics and Statistics is also called ICPMS 2021.

(2) Date

The specific start and ending dates of the event.

(3) Location/Venue

An academic venue is a conference location that plays a vital role in promoting interaction and audience engagement among delegates. Many academic venues offer dedicated residential conference facilities which cover cutting-edge technology, high-quality accommodation and excellent catering.

(4) Themes

Themes are the important issues to be discussed or addressed in the conference.

2) Organizational Information

(1) Conference Sponsors and Organizers

Conference sponsors are the organizations responsible for the financial, technical, publicity, and administrative running of the conference. They can be the initiators of the events or the institutions that pay for all or part of the events. And a conference organizer takes care of planning and executing conferences on behalf of academics, researchers and associations.

(2) Organizing Committee

Establishing a conference organizing committee is one of the first tasks for every conference organizer. Large conferences are often organized by a team of individuals with specific roles and responsibilities. The roles and duties are listed below.

The general chair makes all final decisions regarding the conference, including how other roles and responsibilities are divided.

The program committee, also called the academic committee, paper committee or scientific committee, works together with the general chair. They develop the conference's call for papers and take responsibility for the peer review process and the conference schedule.

The publicity committee takes responsibility for promoting the conference to potential authors, delegates and the media. The members are responsible for releasing the conference's media accounts, and may work with the program committee to develop the call for papers.

The local committee looks after the practical conference arrangements. The members find and suggest venues, take care of the suppliers and logistics and often manage the delegate registration system.

The finance committee takes charge of creating a conference budget, managing expenses and creating financial reports.

The steering committee is responsible for the overall operation of the conference, including appointing the conference's general chair and probably the program chair. The members examine and approve the key ideas of the conference, steer its strategic direction, and may decide where and when the conference takes place each year.

3) Participants Information

(1) Requirements for Attendees

Sometimes eligibility requirements are set in order to make sure the attendees share similar background and pave the way for efficient and focused interaction. The potential conference-goers should check the specifications in advance, to see whether they comply with the specific conditions, for example membership, age or specialization.

(2) Conference VIPs

For a conference, keynote speakers, prominent guests, and industry leaders are the most valuable assets. They can offer what exactly the attendees have registered for—vital early-stage research, discussion opportunities, and professional connections.

4) Paper Submission Information

The submission information describes the types of submissions and the ways to submit a potential participant's work invited for consideration, with essential details like the deadline, length and format attached. The common types are abstracts and the full text of the research papers. Moreover, modes of presentations at the conference will be clarified, notifying whether the attendee needs to present in the plenary sessions or parallel sessions, oral or poster presentations as well as which audio and visual devices should be adopted.

5) Conference Program Information

(1) Conference Brochure

A conference brochure is a paper or document that conveys comprehensive information about the conference to all the people involved. It helps the targeted audiences get the right information concerning the schedule, the venue, the speakers, travel arrangements and other key facts. The informative and persuasive information encourages readers to reserve their

UNIT 9 Identifying International Conference Information

spots so that they can benefit personally or professionally.

(2) Conference Invitation

A conference invitation is written to send an invitation to special guests and participants to an organized conference. The letter should include details about the topic or theme of the forthcoming conference, the venue, the date, the time of the meeting and other important arrangements, which will motivate prospective speakers or chief guests to make a favorable decision about attending the event.

(3) Conference Notice/Call for Papers

The conference notice or announcement sometimes overlaps with the call for papers in that both are written by the organizers with the aim of attracting abstracts or papers all over the research world. They inform the potential participants information like the name, date, venue, organizers and purposes of the conference, but a call for papers is also featured with details about the specific themes, paper or abstract submission, obtaining notification of acceptance, keynote speakers, members of program committee, chairs and so on. The latter offers more comprehensive and detailed information.

>Tasks

1 Work with 2 or 3 students who share similar research interest with you. Search online for a CFP of a forthcoming academic conference in your field. Browse the CFP and answer the following questions:

1. What is the purpose of the conference?
2. When and where is the conference going to take place?
3. How to submit your paper or abstract? And when is the deadline?

2 Discuss with your group members what kind of information do you need to obtain in order to attend an international academic conference?

3 Which facts of information play a crucial role when it is time for you to choose a conference to attend? Make a list of them and explain why.

9.4.2 Major Conference Activities

The activity arrangements may vary from conference to conference, but generally speaking, most academic meetings are featured with plenary meetings, parallel sessions and poster sessions.

1) Plenary Sessions

Plenary sessions are the ones that all participants are present. Keynote speakers, who deliver speeches on a central idea of the conferences, give high-profile presentations in these sessions. As professionals of renown and prestige in the specific field, they address on the common interest of all the attendees and are usually paid by the organizers. A qualified keynote presentation should inspire and unify the attendees with a shared purpose. They should also provide direction for the conference purposes and theme. This establishes the basic tone for the event, which resonates through it. And the conference is hence officially launched.

The plenary presentations often last 60 to 90 minutes and are usually followed by questions and discussions.

2) Parallel Sessions

If the conference is a large one, there will be concurrent events called parallel sessions. Parallel sessions refer to the multiple smaller-scale sessions that occur at the same time. This means that there might be two, four, or even more talks happening simultaneously in different locations. Each session has a focused topic and is prepared for scholars sharing the same specific interest. Speakers at the parallel sessions deliver speeches and share their studies orally and the audience can discuss the related questions with them.

The audience need to plan beforehand to find out when and where the talks they want to attend are being held, and make good use of the conference timetable which will hold all of this information.

3) Poster Sessions

A poster presentation is the presentation of research in the form of paper posters on the walls or boards in a designated area. It can take place in a large hall, several smaller rooms, or on a balcony. As viewers walk by, the presenter should deliver a concise informal talk or conduct a demonstration to communicate his or her study to the audience and then wait for the queries and feedback from them.

Different from the fast pace of a verbal presentation, a poster session allows delegates to study the research information in depth and discuss it with the presenter one by one. Therefore, the presenter is supposed to prepare a well-organized, visually-pleasing poster. It is necessary to consider the audience's interest and decide what information to include first. The presenter then moves on to create the text, graphics as well as format of the poster accordingly.

UNIT 9 Identifying International Conference Information

> Tasks

❶ Answer the following questions.

1. Who usually gives presentations at a plenary meeting?
2. How are parallel sessions organized?
3. How do presenters communicate with the delegates in poster sessions?

❷ Work with a partner and discuss the following question: Among the major activities in an academic conference, which interests you most? And why?

> Language Toolkit

Useful Expressions and Sentence Patterns of Discussing International Conference Activities:

- plenary sessions/meetings
- distinguished guests and outstanding experts of a specific field
- topics of universal significance and general interest
- to learn about the latest trends in the research field
- parallel sessions
- smaller in scale
- more specific research topics
- opportunities to discuss with the presenters
- to probe into the details of the study
- poster sessions
- queries and answers
- informal arrangement
- delegates/attendees drift in and out of each venue freely
- in-depth one on one discussion
- to receive feedback to improve the research work
- I am particularly interested in…because…
- …is particularly important/interesting/attractive to me in that…
- As far as I am concerned, …is a vital factor in selecting academic conferences to

participate.
- The advantages of…include but are not limited to….
- …is definitely advantageous because…
- …has a positive impact/influence/effect on…
- The positive features also include…
- …seems to be equally important.

Reflection & Practice

1. Browse the Internet and find out a CFP and a conference notice, both for international academic conferences in your field. Scan through the documents and make an outline of each. And then share your outlines in a group of 3 to 4 persons, check with each other and work out a final draft of the outline for a CFP and a conference notice respectively.

2. Since networking is one of the key benefits for a conference participant, figure out how to maximize the possibility of networking on the following occasions.

Occasion	Ways of networking
Plenary sessions (as a listener)	
Parallel sessions (as a presenter)	
Parallel sessions (as a listener)	
Poster sessions (as a presenter)	
Poster sessions (as a viewer)	

Unit 10
Making a Paper Presentation

Learning Objectives

- To understand and follow the general structure of a presentation;

- To know the different presentation skills in presentation delivery;

- To practise the common techniques to show your confidence;

- To be able to present research achievements effectively.

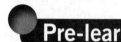

Pre-learning Questions

1. How do you turn a conference paper into a conference presentation?
2. What might be the difficulties you encounter when preparing and delivering a presentation?
3. Do you know how to demonstrate your confidence and communicate your research findings effectively to audience?
4. What are the skills and techniques you can adopt to improve your delivery of a presentation?

To attend to an academic conference, you may be required to write a conference paper and make a presentation on it. Conference papers is a formal academic paper which shares the same conventions and stylistic features of professional papers. To present your conference paper at a presentation session is not the same as to read it word by word. Due to the time limitation, the contents of a paper presentation should be much more concise, removing all but the most essential points—research questions, methods, results and conclusion. In the meanwhile, presentation skills, such as the use of your voice and body language, should be applied. To make a presentation in international academic conferences or other international academic communication activities successfully is not only a great opportunity for you to build and demonstrate your academic confidence, but also an excellent chance to show the images of Chinese researchers in international academic context. In this unit, you will learn the general structure of a formal presentation and skills for preparing and delivering a presentation. Hopefully, you can understand how to turn your paper into a paper presentation and make an effective presentation confidently after studying this unit.

10.1 Structuring a Presentation

Classroom Voice

Laura will deliver a paper presentation 3 weeks later, and now she has been working on it for many days. She has decided the content of her presentation, but she is worrying about its structure, for example, how to start, how to develop the contents logically, and how to end the presentation. She wants to look for suggestions on structuring her presentation.

UNIT 10 Making a Paper Presentation

Instructor's Voice

Every speech, whether long or short, usually consists of three main parts: introduction, main body and conclusion. So does a conference presentation. When outlining your presentation, your goal should be to make the contents structured, logical and easy to follow so that you can communicate your ideas effectively to your audience.

Have you noticed the general structure of academic presentations? Can you tell some effective ways to arrange ideas? Do you know how to start and end a presentation? In this part, the common structure of presentations will be introduced. To facilitate your understanding on each part of the structure, special attention should be paid to their functions and purposes.

10.1.1 Opening

The purpose of the opening is to attract people's attention, and introduce the presenter and the presentation. A strong opening also shows your confidence and the full preparations you made. The most common and traditional contents of an opening are as follows:

1) Attracting Attention and Greeting

When you come to the stage, it is necessary to indicate that the presentation is about to start by using some techniques, like using exclamation, asking questions or declaring the start. Or sometimes remaining silent and waiting until everyone is looking at the stage is also effective in attracting audience's attention. Rushing into talking is usually considered to be lack of confidence and should be, therefore, avoided.

2) Self-introduction or Appreciation

At the beginning of the presentation, normally you need to concisely introduce your name, affiliation, research areas, and academic background etc., so that the audience can know who the you are, how you are qualified and why you are qualified to deliver the presentation.

In a conference presentation, the chair of the session will make a brief complementary introduction to you. Then you should thank the chair and greet the audience rather than repeat a self-introduction when coming to the platform.

If the paper presented has more than one author and you are one of the co-authors who deliver the presentation on behalf of the others, a brief introduction to the other authors and an acknowledgement to their contributions should be made.

3) Introduction to the Topic

You have the responsibility to tell the audience the general topic of the presentation. In some cases, such as an interdisciplinary conference, an explanation or a working definition of the subject should be given to help the audience understand what it is.

For paper presentations, the abstract should be introduced here to give the audience a rough idea of your study, but remember not to read it all, especially when it is very long. Only the key points that indicate the uniqueness of your study such as the research questions, methods and major findings should be presented.

4) Introduction to the Outline

You also have to tell how many sections the presentation has been divided into, what the sections are, and the order of each section. This forecast of the outline is to help the audience understand how the contents are developed, so that during the presentation they can review the outline to follow your talk.

5) Moving to the Main Body

At the end, you should indicate clearly that the opening section has come to an end and the presentation is moving to the main body by saying "Ok, now let's start with the first section on…".

Tasks

1 Watch a video of the opening of a presentation and answer the following questions.

1. What was the topic of the presentation?
2. Why was the presenter qualified to make the presentation?
3. How many sections were covered in his presentation?

2 Watch the video in Task 1 again and take some notes on how he started the presentation and what language expression he used in different parts of the opening, especially how he introduced his topic and outlined the contents.

Contents of the opening	Expressions used in the video
Attracting attention and greeting	
Self-introduction or appreciation	
Introduction to the topic	
Introduction to the outline	
Moving to the main body	

UNIT 10 Making a Paper Presentation

> **Language Toolkit**

Useful Expressions and Sentence Patterns of Opening a Presentation:

1) Attracting Attention

- Well/Right/OK/Err/Good/Fine/Great, …
- Shall we start? / Can we start?
- Let's begin. / Let's get the ball rolling. / Let's get down to business.

2) Greeting

- Hello. / Good morning/afternoon/evening.
- Everyone/Ladies and gentleman/Distinguished guests/fellow colleagues.

3) Self-Introduction

- Let me introduce myself. / I'd like to start by introducing myself.
- My name is XX from XXX Department/group/school/university.
- I am a/an undergraduate/postgraduate/doctoral student (at…).
- I am a researcher from…I've been working on the subject now for…years.
- I'm very glad/pleased to be able to…/ It's an honor to have this opportunity to…/ It's a pleasure to…

4) Extending Thanks

- Thank you, Mr. Chairman (for your kind/warm introduction).
- First of all, I would like to thank our generous host for…

5) Introducing the Topic

- I'm going to talk about/explain/inform you about…
- I'd like to talk about/give you a general introduction about…
- The subject/focus/topic of my presentation today is…
- What I would like to talk to you today is…

6) Introducing the Presentation

- I've divided my presentation into XX parts/sections. They are…
- My presentation today will cover the following XX sections…
- We will talk about this topic from the following XX parts…
- Firstly…Secondly…Thirdly…

- First/First of all…Next…Then…Finally/Lastly/Last of all…

7) Moving to the Main Body

- Now, let's start from the first section…
- Let's start by introducing/explaining/exploring/analyzing…
- Now let's turn to Point One.

10.1.2 Main Body

The main body is the most important part of a presentation where the content should be developed clearly and logically. In this part, both the content and the approach play a crucial role in the effectiveness of communicating the presenter's ideas to the audience. If the ideas are arranged in a cohesive and clear way, the audience can easily grasp the key points and be interested. Otherwise, they will get lost in the details and quickly lose their interests. There are several common approaches to sequence ideas:

- chronological way;
- general to specific;
- known to unknown;
- accepted to controversial;
- cause and effect;
- problem and solution;
- most important to least important.

According to the content and focus of a presentation, these approaches should be employed alone or together.

For paper presentations, its main body follows a relatively fixed structure of papers as shown in Table 10.1:

Table 10.1 Structure of Paper Presentations

1. Motivation and problem statement	Briefly introduce the background, why the study is conducted and what goals to achieve.
2. Related works	Briefly introduce this part but remember to refer people to this section in the paper.
3. Methods	Briefly explain the methods applied and how the research was conducted. Cover this part quickly in short talks and refer people to the details in the paper.

(cont.)

4. Results	Present key results with implications. This is the most important part of the talk. Do not cover all the results. Cover only the key result well.
4. Summary	Summarize the study along with its limitations and/or the suggestions on future works. It is different from the summary of a presentation.

> Tasks

❶ **Plan a short presentation on your major and decide what your main message will be. Then write an outline of the main body of your presentation. Make very short notes under each of the headings like the following:**

- Main Point 1+Details (Example/Comment/Explanation)
- Main Point 2+Details (Example/Comment/Explanation)

...

❷ **Think about the approaches you could take to introduce the main points and the details. Note down your ideas and reasons for your choice. Then, exchange your outline with each other in pairs and try to make some suggestions to improve it.**

10.1.3 Ending

The principal function of the ending is to summarize and restate the key points. Its common procedure is as follows:

1) Indicating the End

To transfer from the main body to the conclusion, you need to tell the audience clearly that you are heading to the end of the presentation by saying "To conclude…" or "To recap the main points…" to bring them a sense of finality.

2) Summarizing the Main Points

The summary is to review the main contents that your audience are expected to remember. It is the last chance to reinforce the audience's impression on the main ideas and stress the focuses. You should conclude how many sections you presented, what these sections were, and the key points of each section.

3) Thanking the Audience for Listening

It is a convention and etiquette to say thank you at the end of all the academic communication activities, so don't forget to thank the audience for listening. It is to show your gratitude and indicate that the whole presentation is over.

4) Inviting Questions or Comments

After the presentation, a Q & A or a discussion section will be held to allow the audience to communicate with the presenter. Before leaving the stage, you should tell the audience that the Q & A session is open and they are welcome to ask questions or make comments. Sometimes the session chair will invite the audience for the presenter.

> Tasks

❶ Read the transcript of the conclusion part of a presentation on the impacts of tourism industry on destination countries. Make an outline according to the conclusion part.

OK, let me recap the main points. In my presentation today, I discussed the impacts of tourism industry on destination countries from three main aspects. Firstly, I explained its social impacts on the destination countries, especially in developing countries. On the one hand, it can increase the variety of jobs available in their job markets, and provide new range of business opportunities. On the other hand, however, it may lead to price inflation in the destinations. For example, the situations in Hainan Island and Turkey. Secondly, I talked about some influences of tourism on the cultural aspects. For example, new patterns of dress and behavior of the tourists may lead to some cultural conflicts with the local cultural conventions. But, at the same time, with the increasing number of tourists, the demand for traditional crafts and ritual will increase, which may contribute to the growth of these markets in the destination countries. Thirdly, I discussed its impacts from environmental aspects. Among them, the most important ones are the influences of tourist facilities on the natural habitat and the pressure posed on the limited resources of the destination, like water and food. I think now you can see how tourism industry influences the destination countries both positively and negatively. Thanks for listening. Now, I'm happy to deal with any questions you have.

❷ Use the outline you made in Task 1 of Section 10.1.2 to make a clear and strong conclusion of your presentation in groups of 4 or 5 students who are in the same major as you are. Show your outline while speaking and ask for their feedback.

UNIT 10 Making a Paper Presentation

> **Language Toolkit**

Useful Expressions and Sentence Patterns of Delivering the Ending:

1) Indicating You Are About to Finish

- To conclude/sum up…
- So, in conclusion/summary…
- That brings me to my conclusion/summary…
- I'd like to conclude/summarize by saying…
- OK, to recap the main points…

2) Summarizing Your Main Points

- In my presentation today, I talked about…from…aspects. In the first section, I introduced…In the second section, I explained…In the last section, I discussed…
- My presentation today introduced…in…sections. They are firstly…Secondly…Thirdly…

3) Thanking Your Audience for Listening

- Thank you for listening/for your patience/attention.
- I'd like to thank you all for coming to listen to my talk.

4) Inviting Questions or Comments

- Now, if there are any questions?
- Are there any questions?
- Do you have any questions or comments?
- Now, I'm happy to deal with any questions…

> **Reflection & Practice**

1. What are the differences between introducing the outline in the opening and summarizing the contents in the ending of your presentation?

2. Watch some conference presentations with a topic related to your major, and analyze their structures. Then find students who are in the same or similar majors and discuss in groups:

    1) Opening
    - How did they start their presentation?
    - Did they use any other approaches of starting the presentations?

2) Main Body

- What are the approaches they adopted in developing the contents? Have you noticed any signposting language to signal the transition of sections?

- How did they arrange the time allocation for the main body? What is the most important part of their main body? What kind of content do you think should be the focus of the main body? Why?

3) Conclusion

- How did they summarize the key points? Did they use the signal language at the start of the conclusion? Did they summarize their main points clearly? What linkages did they use in connecting the points?

3. Collect one conference paper in your research field. You are going to make a presentation on it at the end of this unit. Its length should be no more than 10 minutes. You can now structure the contents of your presentation according to what you learnt in this part and make an outline.

10.2 Preparing a Presentation

Classroom Voice

Cara has been working on her paper presentation for many days. Though she's done a lot of works, she still feels anxious, because she doesn't know if she has done enough for the preparation. And she seems to have problems in designing her PowerPoint slides. That is, she has copied all the information she wants to present from her conference paper and pasted them directly on her slides.

Instructor's Voice

Preparation of a presentation involves lots of works. To get yourself ready for the delivery, many factors should be considered such as the contents, the audience, the presentation place, the design of visual aids and so on. Therefore, it normally involves a long preparation time of many different stages with many aspects to consider.

Conference presentations nowadays are mostly PowerPoint presentations, so you need to consider how to arrange the contents of the slides to facilitate your audience's understanding of your presentation. This part will introduce the works you need to do before delivering a presentation with a focus on designing the PowerPoint to guide your preparation.

10.2.1 Preparation Procedure

Good preparation leads to an effective presentation. Although it is very energy-demanding and time-consuming, it is worthwhile to do so. There are a number of aspects that you need to consider when preparing a presentation. The common steps in the preparation have been summarized in Table 10.2:

Table 10.2 Common Steps in the Preparation Procedure

Steps	Things to do	Functions
Set the objective	Think about: - What I want to do by delivering the presentation; - What the audience are expected to do at the end of the presentation.	- To help identify the focus.
Analyze the audience	Analyze the audience's: - Background (e.g. nationality, occupation, age, gender, etc.); - Knowledge of the topic (/level of understanding); - Interests; - English proficiency.	- To tailor the contents, way of delivering and language (expression).
Decide the outline	- Follow the common structure of presentations; - Find the proper ways to organize ideas.	- To help organize the contents logically.
Write the scripts	- Write exact words and sentences to be used in the presentation, especially in the opening and conclusion; - Choose the right style of language.	- To make sure what to talk and how to talk.
Design the visual aids	- Design the PowerPoint slides (font, word size, color, background, etc.); - Choose the proper types of visual aids (e.g. picture, photo, table, graph, text, etc.) according to the features of the information presented.	- To facilitate audience's understanding; - To make the talk easy to follow.

(cont.)

Steps	Things to do	Functions
Practise	- Practise with the PowerPoint slides; - Practise in front of a mirror; - Practise in front of a real audience.	- To check the contents, language expression, PPT slides, and body language; - To get real feedback in every aspect.
Know the presentation area	Know the place to deliver the presentation: - Find how big the room is & how many people there will be; - Check the facilities in the room that can be used.	- To decide whether or not a microphone is needed; - To make sure the equipment works well and know how to use them.
Rehearse	- Come to the presentation in advance on the due date; - Rehearse the whole presentation for at least once.	- To check the equipment, facilities and area; - To help calm down and relax.

❯ Tasks

❶ Decide if the following suggestions on preparing a presentation is helpful or not, and explain why.

A. The more visual aids you use, the more effective your communication of ideas will be.

B. To write the transcripts of a paper presentation is to pick out sentences from your conference paper, so you don't actually need to write them at all.

C. You should use the transcripts to help you remind the points and avoid forgetting the contents.

D. You should prepare your speech using complex sentence patterns and terminologies to show your academic ability.

E. The main objective of your paper presentation should be to inform the audience of your research and let them read your paper.

F. The best way to practise your presentation is to practise with your PowerPoint slides in front of real audience like your friends or classmates.

UNIT 10 Making a Paper Presentation

G. Special attention should be paid to the physical setting of the presentation area such as the room temperature, the lighting, and the sound of the microphone and computer system.

H. You can use notecards with the structure and the unfamiliar points or pronunciation on it when practicing the contents.

I. To design the PowerPoint is to copy and paste sentences or paragraphs from your conference paper.

J. It is necessary to recite your introduction and conclusion in preparation.

❷ Work in groups and summarize a list of suggestions you can follow at each stage of the preparation.

Stage of preparing a presentation	Suggestions
Set the objective	
Analyze the audience	
Decide the outline	
Write the scripts	
Design visual aids	
Practice	
Know the presentation area	
Rehearse	

〉Language Toolkit

Useful Sentence Patterns of Discussing the Preparation of Presentations:

- The general/common process/procedure/steps of preparing a presentation includes…
- First of all, before we do anything for the presentation, we need to set/decide/consider/think about/know the objective/aim/purpose/goal of our presentation.
- Also, it is necessary to tailor/adjust/arrange/design the contents of your presentation (according) to your audience's level/interests/needs/language proficiency.

  While you are practicing, keep an eye on/develop a sense of/watch the time.

211

10.2.2 PowerPoint Design

- The slides should be attractive but not distractingly decorated. Don't be tempted to make the slides too "busy". Select a proper template and limit the number of visual aids. Avoid anything that is not related. Use short text with not too many words. List only the bullet points and a separate line for each point. Normally six lines of text per slide is enough, otherwise, it will be unreadable.

- The font should be at least 24 points or larger in order to make sure it can be read by all the audience even people at the back of the room. Use the sans-serif fonts like Arial that be read easily from a distance.

- Choose the colors carefully. Use contrasting colors for the text and the background. Be careful with reds and greens, since some people have difficulty in reading them. Also, avoid using too many colors on one slide, which will be very distractive.

- Each slide and each graphic should have a title, so that the audience can recognize what they are looking at. Normally the minimal size for the headings should be 32 points or larger.

- At the end of the presentation while answering questions, you can leave up a contact information slide containing the name, e-mail, address, and website URL related to the talk if there is one, so that if the audience wants to contact for details or future cooperation, they can find the presenter.

- Keep it academic. Check spelling and grammar mistakes. If the graphics or the text is taken from other sources, remember to give acknowledgement to the sources and put it in the reference page on the last slide.

- Do not make it too technical. The more advanced technologies are applied, the more likely there are "technical problems". Check the compatibility when the file is saved. Always send a copy of the presentation to the conference organizer in advance so it can be loaded and tested. Meanwhile, prepare backups like a USB, the network disk, email, or some other common information storage formats.

▶ Tasks

❶ Discuss in groups what would be the best kind of visual aid to use.

A. to show the wireless charging system for mobile phones

B. to show the number of safety accidents in China from 1990 to now

C. to compare the differences and similarities of two technical terms

UNIT 10 Making a Paper Presentation

  D. to compare GDP of Asia countries, including China, Japan, South Korea, and India, in 2020

  E. to show the percentages of coal, oil, gas, wind energy and solar energy in national energy consumption of 2019

❷ **Study the slides below prepared by a student about climate change and environment protection. Think about any changes you would make to the individual slides according what you learnt in this part.**

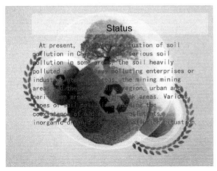
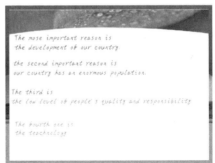

› Language Toolkit

Useful Sentence Patterns of Giving Suggestions on the PowerPoint Design:

- It is important to use/adopt/design/choose proper visual aids in your presentation.
- The common visual aids include…
- The most commonly used visual aid is…
- One of the principles to follow when designing the visual aids should/can be…
- Make sure you avoid anything that will distract your audience.
- …may influence your professional image.
- The contents of the slides should be well-prepared/well-designed in…

- Sometimes, you need to limit the number of visual aids and colors.
- The headings and…should be written in upper case/capital letter/lower case.
- Unnecessary details/information, such as…must be eliminated.
- Then, you should backup your PowerPoint to avoid problems like…
- Also, you can save your files in different storage medias.

Reflection & Practice

1. You are going to deliver a presentation on the conference paper you found in Reflection & Practice 1 of Section 10.1. Finish the presentation preparation checklist below according to your own situation, analyzing aspects including objective, audience, outline, presentation area, etc.

Preparation Checklist

Questions to think	My ideas
What is the aim?	
What is my title?	
Who am I speaking to?	
What are the main points I want to make?	
What should be the focuses of my presentation?	
How long will it be?	
How many audiences do I have?	
Where am I going to make the presentation? How big is the room?	
What equipment is there? What equipment do I need? Do they work?	
Am I going to need a black or white board? Have I got a chalk or a pen?	
Where am I going to put my notes?	
Do I need to dim the lights or draw the curtains?	
What time of day is it?	
Am I dressed appropriately?	

2. Go on with your preparation for the paper presentation on the conference paper in Reflection & Practice 1 of Section 10.1. This time, design the PowerPoint slides according to your contents. Remember to follow the general guidelines and use graphics where appropriate.

10.3 Delivering a Presentation

Classroom Voice

To get herself ready for the coming presentation, Carol delivered it to some of her "critical friends". They suggested that she should be more confident. They also found she spoke in a flat monotone, which made her talk boring and dull. Now she is eager to solve these problems but she doesn't know how.

Instructor's Voice

The delivery of a presentation is as important as its content and structure. If the audience cannot understand what the presenter is saying, then the content will be useless. The delivery is about not only verbal expression, but also many other important skills including voice, body language, visual aids, organization and style of delivery.

Without these presentation skills, you may have the same problems as Carol does and these eventually lead to failure in presentation. So what are the skills used by most presenters, especially the advanced presenters? What verbal expression can you use during the presentation? This part will elaborate on these skills and verbal expressions in hopes of facilitating your presentation delivery and enhance your public speaking ability.

10.3.1 Presentation Skills

1) Minding the Body Language

In public speaking, how a presenter behaves will significantly influence the impression of the audience. Body language, including posture, gesture, eye-contact and movement, plays an essential role in showing your confidence and delivering an effective presentation.

(1) Posture

Posture conveys a message to the audience about whether or not a presenter is confident. You should stand up straight with an erect and relaxed posture to show the audience that you are confident. Hands in the pocket, crossing the arms or hiding behind the computer are considered as improper postures and should be strictly avoided.

(2) Gesture

Gesture refers to the movement of someone's hands and arms. Using natural gestures according to the contents of the presentation can not only indicate the presenter's confidence, but also help to emphasize a point and draw audience's attention. But be careful to keep it within the movement of your elbows, otherwise it will be too exaggerated.

(3) Eye-contact

Effective eye-contact is to cast the presenter's eyes slowly from person to person and from one side of the room to another. Effective eye-contact can promote the audience's involvement by giving them the feeling that you are speaking to them personally. You can also check the audience's feedback by making eye-contact with them. However, staring at one or two particular persons in one direction is not appropriate when making eye-contact.

(4) Movement

A presenter can and should have some movements while talking, but don't move forth and back or sway from side to side. It will strongly distract the audience from the talk. You can walk to the screen when referring to a particular point on a slide, and move back after finishing that point. If there are more than one point to show on one single slide, you should stay at the screen until all of those points have been explained, rather than move back and forth for several times.

2) Making Full Use of Voice

In presentation, voice can do many things. If a presenter talks in monotone of voice at the same pace, audience will feel bored and find it hard to follow the points.

(1) Volume

Presenters should speak loud enough to allow everyone in the room hear them clearly. If the audience cannot hear what you are saying, it will be impossible for them to understand you. Also, variations of your volume indicate a stress or an attempt to attract attention. For example, when emphasizing a point, you can raise your volume and speak louder to indicate your audience that you are making a focus.

(2) Pace

Presenters should avoid speaking too quickly or too slowly when speaking to the public. It is suggested to speak a little slower in the presentation than you use to be, especially when speaking at international conferences where the audience may be non-native English speakers. Also, remember to speak a bit slower if you want to stress an important point.

(3) Tone

Different tones indicate different emotions and emphases. Usually, higher tone suggests

UNIT 10 Making a Paper Presentation

a stress, questioning and feelings like passion, anger, and excitement, while low tone reveals depressed feelings, certainty or seriousness. In paper presentation, you need to vary tones according to different cases. For example, you can raise your tone to stress a point or raise a question, or you can speak at a lower tone to show your certainty and confidence.

(4) Pronunciation

Incorrect and inaccurate pronunciation will greatly distract the audience and block their understanding, so make sure the pronunciation of each word is correct, especially those of the key words which are used a lot in the presentation.

3) Using Notecards

It is common that presenters use notes to remind themselves of the important points or anything that may be easily forgotten during the presentation. The notes should be written in the order they appear in the content, with words that are large enough to read easily. The pronunciations of the unfamiliar words, confusing points or anything you are not quite confident with can be written in the notes. However, you should make sure you do not stare at them all the time. Look down at the notes only when it is necessary, then look up and speak to the audience.

> Tasks

❶ Work with a partner on the following bad behaviors that should be avoided when delivering a presentation. Discuss why these behaviors are bad and give some suggestions to improve.

A. Put your hands in your pocket.

B. Turn your back to your audience.

C. Stare at only one of your audience.

D. Look at your feet or the celling.

E. Walk around all the time.

F. Hide behind the computer.

G. Play your hair, or touch your nose.

H. Keep your voice at one tone.

I. Speak too fast.

J. Read your PPT or notes in your hand.

❷ Prepare a notecard according to the text below and try to speak without looking at the original text.

I think a **real** business person, a **real** entrepreneur, not only knows how to **make money**, but how to **spend money**. And we do **not live for** money, we do **not work for** money. When you have **one million**, that is **your** money. When you have **ten million**, maybe, the **problem comes**. When you have **a hundred million** dollars, I think that is **not your** money. That's the **trust the society gives to you**. They **believe** that you can **spend** the money **better**, you can **use** the money **better**. So, a **real** businessperson is **not** making money by **making use of** the **mistakes** or **social problems**. A **real** businessperson makes the money by **solving the social problems** for the others.

(Source: Ma Yun's speech in the Commencement Ceremony of Hong Kong University in 2018)

Practise with your partners and you should:

- only rely on your notecard;
- rephrase it if needed;
- use your voice properly to emphasize the bolded words;
- mind your body language.

10.3.2 Verbal Expressions

1) Signposting Language

Signposting language is like the signposts that can be seen on the streets, which tell people where they are and where they are going. You can use signposting expressions like "Now, let's start from the first section." or "Having explained that, now let's move to the next section.", "That brings me to the last section of my presentation." in between different sections of your presentation to indicate that you are moving from one section to another. Effective use of the signposting language will guide the audience through the presentation and help them follow the structure.

2) Emphasizing

Apart from using your voice and body language, you can emphasize a point by using emphatic sentence structures and emphatic words to make the point more forceful, or repeating the key points by rephrasing them. Sometimes explicit language instructions like "This is the point I'd like to stress on" can also be a straightforward way of emphasizing.

3) Referring to Visual Aids

When referring to the visual aids, you need to explain them and expand a little bit, rather than read the headings, or say "This is a table/photo/diagram." and let the audience read by themselves. Your audience will not be able to understand these graphics immediately unless you explain them. Therefore, you should introduce what the graphic is by telling its title "This is a table/photo/chart/graph of …", and then go on to elaborate it with more details by saying "As you can see, at the top/bottom, …" or "In the first/second/third column, …".

Tasks

1 Watch a video of a lecture on the coverage of celebrities on mass media and answer the following questions.

1. How many main points did professor cover in the lecture?
2. How did the professor transfer the sections?
3. What signposting language did he use?

(Source: "Lecture Ready 1", retrieved from bilibili website)

2 Watch the video in Task 1 again and this time you are expected to see and notice the way how the professor introduced the bar chart on Celebrity Coverage in *News Magazines* from 1980-2003 in the USA and explained it with details. Write down your ideas and discuss with your partners.

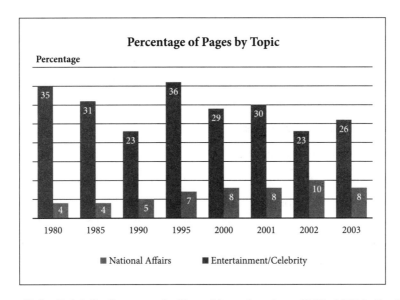

Figure 10.1 Celebrity Coverage in *News Magazines* from 1980–2003 in the USA

(Source: "Lecture Ready 1", retrieved from bilibili website)

❸ **The bar chart below shows the growth of renewable power capacity from 2016 to 2020. Take turns to present the chart in pairs, and then check your partner's understanding of your talk.**

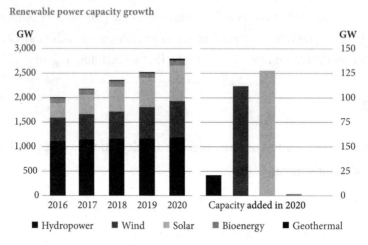

Figure 10.2　The Growth of Renewable Power Capacity from 2016 to 2020

(Source: IRENA. 2021. Renewable capacity highlights.03-31.From IRENA website.)

〉 Language Toolkit

Useful Expressions and Sentences to Be Used in the Main Body of a Presentation:

1) Emphasizing

- It is…that….
- Since this is a key problem, I'd like to go into some detail.
- Please allow me to deal with this matter more extensively.
- What is very significant is…
- I'd like to emphasize the fact that…
- I'd like to stress the importance of…
- To highlight…
- What we need to focus on…

2) Signposting Language

- Let's start by/from…
- I'd like to move on to…

UNIT 10 Making a Paper Presentation

- Let's move/go on/turn to… (the second/third/fourth…of my presentation).
- That brings us to…
- Now we come to the second/third/fourth…
- So that has dealt with the X aspect…Now, we move on to…
- Having explained/considered…, it's time to go into…

3) Referring to Visual Aids

Introducing the Visual Aids

- You can see here…
- Here you can see…
- If we look at this slide…
- Here are the data from…
- This table/line graph/diagram/pie chart/bar chart shows …
- Let's look at the screen…

Locating a Point on a Slide

- On the left/right side…
- At the top/bottom…
- In the first/second…column/line…

❯ Reflection & Practice

1. Find videos of Chinese and foreign researchers who made confident and effective presentations. Observe how they used their voice, body language, and verbal expressions to make their presentations easy-to-follow. Also, you should note down any techniques they applied to show their confidence.

2. Make a paper presentation on the conference paper in Reflection & Practice 1 of Section 10.1. The length should be no more than 10 minutes. Make sure that you follow the common structure of a formal presentation and the presentation skills. Also, you should get ready to answer audience's questions after your delivering.

3. While listening to other students' presentations, you should take notes and ask related questions. After each presentation, you are expected to summarize their performance according the following aspects.

	Score (0-10)	Problems you noticed	What impressed you
1. Opening			
- Greeting & Self-introduction - Introduction to the presentation (topic, objective, outline, length) - Inviting questions - Transferring to the main body			
2. Conclusion	Score (0-10)	Problems you noticed	What impressed you
- Signaling the ending - Summarizing main points - Thanking audience - Inviting questions			
3. Main body	Score (0-10)	Problems you noticed	What impressed you
- Signposting language - Keeping audience attention - Selection of contents - References - Accuracy			
4. Body language	Score (0-10)	Problems you noticed	What impressed you
- Eye-contact - Posture - Movement - Gesture			
5. Voice	Score (0-10)	Problems you noticed	What impressed you
- Loud - Pace - Tone - Pronunciation			

(cont.)

6. PowerPoint design	Score (0-10)	Problems you noticed	What impressed you
- Clear to read (font, color, background) - Title page, content page, conclusion page, reference page - Heading for each slide - Listing only bullet points - Using graphics where necessary - Accuracy			

7. Overall	Score (0-10)	Problems you noticed	What impressed you
- Well-prepared - Confident - Read, recite or speak from points - Understandable - Time management - Academic style			

4. Collect audience's feedback or comments on your presentation, and write a self-evaluation report on your own performance or the problems you had in preparing and delivering the presentation.

Unit 11
Initiating Free Exchanges with Academics

Learning Objectives

- To understand the importance of free exchange with academics and professionals;

- To obtain the skills to start a talk with academics;

- To talk effectively with academics;

- To actively participate in academic activities.

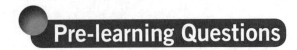

Pre-learning Questions

1. Why do we need free exchanges with academics?
2. Have you ever tried to make any free exchanges with academics?

In this unit, we are going to learn how to make free exchange with professionals and obtain the related communicativetalking skills.

11.1 Preparing a Talk with Professionals

Classroom Voice

Emily has been studying in this university as a graduate student for several months. In her daily academic study, she has met the situation that she is supposed to choose a topic as her essential research direction but she doesn't know what to start with. So she has to make a decision to turn to others for help.

Instructor's Voice

Communication is a key to the success in everything, especially in academic study. An international conference provides an opportunity for extensive communication, which can be free exchange with academics, especially with those professionals and scholars in different fields. Actually, you need to get a right chance to start a talk with them, seek out feedback from them, and try to deepen your talk.

It's better for you to grasp more chances to talk to them. And while talking with them, a sincere advice may be useful for you to always remember in mind: please be open to new comments, criticism and be honest with those scholars about your struggles and concerns.

To improve your talk and learn from others is one of the essential purposes of participating in an international conference. Take full advantages of your talking experience and ask the professionals about their background, and think about a question about how they prepare for their academic fields and how they develop their own academic knowledge. You will learn lots of valuable experiences from them that you are probably unable to get in your own laboratory. Enjoy yourself and learn as much as you can during the talking. Go to start a talk and accept any new learning opportunity while they talk to you. The more exposure you have, the more certainty you will get when you develop academic field on your own.

Opportunities favor prepared minds. If you want to start a talk with professionals smoothly, well-preparation is necessary.

11.1.1 Topic Choosing

A professional or supervisor sometimes specifies a broad academic area. He or she may assign a particular topic, or at least provide a list of possible topics in a conference. You should begin to consider possible topics as soon as you get information of the conference, even before the conference begins. You'd better compile a list of possible topics early in your daily academic study as your future thesis or dissertation as soon as you start your study as a graduate student.

Even in some academic fields that seem to be covered by some other professionals or scholars, possibilities can often be found for further research. Supervisors often suggest undiscussed areas of inquiry or unresolved converses as your analyzing work in the laboratory, but this kind of information isn't suitable for you to discuss with other academics in a conference. You need to choose some relevant topics with a certain professional which is supposed to be helpful to your future research.

> **Task**

In your daily academic study, have you ever met the situation that you had to choose a topic as your essential research field but you didn't know how to start it? Could you share your experience and describe it in details? What did you do at that time? Have you overcome it and what did you do? Make a problem-solve list and discuss it with your partner.

	Problems	Solutions
1.		
2.		
3.		
4.		
...		...

11.1.2 Information Collecting

Information collecting is the first step pf any analyses in your graduate. Here you can divide collection of information into two parts. First, you need to create a working bibliography for your own research, and then, you need to know more about the professional who you intend to talk in the conference.

Take down as much information as you can find. When you look in indexes and other bibliography, you may want to take all the relevant information or messages, and search their resources. It's the primary task for your academic research. But it's not as simple as it looks like. You should keep in mind that bibliographies or lists of cited works contain the following information of books, such as the author's name, the title and subtitle, the editor or translator, even the edition. Taking an article as an example, you need to require the name of journal, the volume, the publican date, and inclusive page numbers. If you found all of this information about those potential source, you would be able to complete the entry for bibliographies. And it may be a start of your analysis.

It also accompanies another work. The one in the know will be the one defending victory at last. To know more about a certain professional is taking a short cut in your talking. It's a subtle task for you to balance what you have known and what you want to know. No matter how much thought you put into predicting the professional, your own thought and ideas will be the basement supporting the talk. Now you need to organize your ideas and outlines.

Task

Nowadays, there are so many electronic sources to collect information, particularly information networks and online databases. Have you got some useful electronic sources online? Could you share them with your classmates? You may follow useful expression below.

Useful Expressions and Sentence Patterns of Greeting:	
For example, …	Think of…
Let's say…	You might…like this
Here is an example…	Recently, I…
Let's start…	Once…, you…
That's the first…	At last/Finally…

11.1.3 Idea Organizing and Outlining

While using the information which you've collected, it's necessary for you to develop an outline to organize your ideas. A well-organized outline will show your main ideas about the talking topic and the discussing order in which you will obey.

UNIT 11 Initiating Free Exchanges with Academics

Here are some suggestions for you to follow to organize your ideas as the first step:

- write down all the main ideas;
- list the subordinate ideas below the main ideas;
- avoid any repeated ideas.

Following those ideas that you put up above, you will develop an outline. An outline must have a general but logical description, a schematic summary, an organized pattern and a conceptual design of your academic work.

In order to get the well-organized outline, you should:

- choose essential ideas that it's useful in your talk;
- integrate those ideas into a logical group;
- arrange supporting materials step by step from general to specific;
- create absorbing highlights in your talking materials.

And an outline has a balanced structure based on the principle as follows:

- parallelism;
- coordination;
- subordination;
- division.

〉Task

It's said that parallelism, the interpretation of scripture by means of scripture, is a corollary of the belief in the unity of scripture. How do we understand it and use it in our outline? Discuss with your partner and fill the blank of an outline.

Main Ideas	1.	2.		
Supporting materials	1.	2.	3.	4.
Subordinate ideas	1.	2.	3.	
Supporting materials	1.	2.	3.	4.
…	…	…	…	…

11.2 Starting a Talk with Professionals

Classroom Voice

It's the first time that Emily gets a chance to attend an international academic conference. Luckily, she finds a professor who she has admired for a long time and read almost every paper of her publication. It's a convention to have a tea break in a conference. Is it suitable for her to start a talk with professionals during the tea-break? Is it an appropriate occasion?

Instructor's Voice

In a conference, especially an international conference, there are various forms of activities in it, apart from formal activities, including other activities such as informal meetings, exhibitions, and visits.

For example, the communication may be conducted between the professionals and the conference presenters in the interval between sessions.

As we all know, it's undoubtedly beneficial to have a talk with academics. But the questions are coming: What occasion is suitable to start a talk? How to start a talk with them?

11.2.1 Talking with Familiar Professionals

It's simple to talk with an acquaintance. The more familiar with the professional you are, the simpler talk you will start. It tends to start the talk directly and politely with your prepared topics.

> Task

Professor Wang is an alumnus who shares the same major as you. And he was a year ahead of your supervisor. Though daily connection by e-mail, it's happened that you meet him in an international conference. How could you start your talk with him? Make a role play with your partner.

Useful Expressions and Sentence Patterns of Giving Examples	
Good morning/afternoon, Mr./Mrs.…	Good day Sir/Madam…
Nice to meet you here.	It's my honor to meet you here.
How are you today?	How are you doing?
Since we met last time, I …	It's a long time for us to meet each other.

11.2.2 Talking with Strangers

It's said that well begun is half done. The key to starting a talk with stranger is the opening introduction.

There is usually no time limit on how long an opening introduction should be, but always remember: be brief. If you only have five minutes to talk, just like a short discussion, don't go on more than two minutes. Within the two minutes' introduction, it's the essential that you need to make the professional known who you are, what you want to talk and what is your main concern. Language should be precise and clear in expressions and warm-hearted in emotion. And try to be sincere and make them feel comfortable. Don't be nervous, just as you are talking with friend at home.

> Task

Professor Johnson is a professor from a very famous university who majors in the same as you are. You have prepared a lot to talk with him. Could you start your talk suitably and bravely? Make a role play with your partner.

Useful Expressions and Sentence Patterns of Self-introduction:
Excuse me, …
Would I have the honor to talk with…?
My name is…a…(student) from…(university). My supervisor is…
Perhaps I would have the chance to …
You are so kind if you would spare me a few minutes to …

11.3 Deepening the Topic

Classroom Voice

It involves many factors about how to deepen the topic in a talk, and it's also a complicated problem bothering those new society comers especially the ones in academic world. Given what Emily has learned, she has made a full preparation for the talking partners—those professionals or scholars, and has already got appointing ideas with deep thought. But now she confronts some new problems about how to talk politely and euphemistically and how to dispute about different opinions.

Instructor's Voice

Here are some expressions for you:

- May I trouble you with more questions?
- I was wondering if I could ask more questions about…
- Could I ask you a couple of questions to have a better look into…?
- I'd like to ask you the following question concerning an early part of your speech that…
- Thank you for your explanation about the positive part of the theory so far. Would you like to give us an example of a negative one if any?
- Interesting points you mentioned stimulate me in many ways. Well, would you elaborate a little more on the first two points?
- Could you be more specific in…?
- Could you enhance your opinions of…?
- I'm very interested in hearing your presentation today on…Would you please say a few words about…?

However, free exchange may not continue as smoothly as you imagine. As young researchers, you will easily let your mind slip through their fingers when you hear the negative voices especially from those professionals you've admired most. Sometimes you would lose control and make the free exchange into a dispute, even a debate. When realizing it, your gruffness will give way to embarrassment. However, it's not the end of the world. Learning from those disputations will undoubtedly enhance your critical thinking abilities. And therefore, disputing or debating with others effectively and politely is the key point you would always remember in your mind. Disputing or debating will develop you applied skills including oral English communication, professionalism and even collaboration. But, it's the time of free exchange, not a debate that you must win. You can argue with them to depend your academic research or findings in a much softer and more elegant way.

Arguments and argumentation are tools primarily used here. There are three elements here for you to control your free exchange in arguments, apart from disputations or debates. First, claim your main ideas or conclusions of your academic research or findings. No matter what they agree it or not, you must make your points scientific and logical. Then you move on to support your claim with stable evidence system with any information on which the claim rests. Now the argument is on your hand but everything is unsettled. As a wonderful ending, you should create a link between the evidence and the claim. It may be a statement that creates a bridge between the professionals and you because you will realize that a successful argument is to reach a consensus instead of denying any part of it.

UNIT 11 Initiating Free Exchanges with Academics

> Task

Make a role play with your partner. Set a topic that you will discuss and one party acts as a graduate and the other plays as a professional. Make a list of sentence patterns that may be used in this context.

Sentence patterns	Situations	Meanings	How to use
I wonder if I could…			
I suppose/think/guess…			
I do agree with much of what you said, but…			
Since I've done this experiment, I hope…			
Now that you've known what I've done on this subject, could I have your comment on…?			
…	…	…	…

11.4 Shifting the Topic

Classroom Voice

In a conference Emily participated, professional may not be left alone for Emily to talk to. So when Emily grasps a chance to start a talk, she may confront a group of professionals instead of the very professor she wants to talk with. In this situation, it's impolite to query a certain person closely. She should have the ability to shift the topics between them. And she should also understand that there are no perfect things and any serious issues would arise during the talk. So she should get ready to shift the topic, no matter natural shifting, or intended shifting, from one professional to another, or even from one topic to another new one.

Instructor's Voice

No one is perfect. Practice makes perfect, but it doesn't mean there are no mistakes at all. Apologizing is needed to be prepared here. An apology is an act of saying that you are sorry for something wrong you have done. But it's not always easy to say sorry only. Polite behavior with good manners sometimes will be much better than words.

If you wish to shift a topic gently, you must be sure to adopt the proper methods and polite expressions. Here are some examples for you:

- Professor A has mentioned very briefly that he used to two experiments that were the same. Professor B, would you please elaborate on this point?
- I'm still confused about the relationship between…and…that Professor A mentioned. Professor B, what's your opinions about it?
- I'm very keen on what Professor A says about….And I remember I've read a paper of Professor B that mentioned an experiment to get a peak date. Professor B, would you be so kind to give me more information about the method of your experiment?

❯ Task

Some Chinese conference-participants are called silent-elite, who like to stay together during the conference, quietly listening instead of actively discussing. What do you think about this phenomenon? Give your comments about it and set up your argument based on your own experiences or examples.

> When you attend the international conference, will you just be a quiet listener?

> Have you met this kind of situation? What reasons do you think are responsible for those?

> What should we do to change these situation? Could you give us detailed steps one by one?

❯ Reflection & Practice

1. After learning this part, could you describe what situations participants at an international conference would talk with each other?
2. If you have already started a talk with an academic, how can you continue this free talk smoothly?
3. It's said that being polite and thoughtful is especially important during these free talk with academics. Do you have any secrets of success to share with us?

Unit 12
Presiding over a Session

📝 Learning Objectives

- To understand what to prepare before a session you are going to chair;

- To know how to start a session as the presider;

- To master how to introduce and thank the speakers appropriately;

- To be familiar with how to manage the interaction between the audience and the speakers;

- To perceive the importance of the presider's role and the basic skills to minimize the conflicts in a meeting.

Pre-learning Questions

1. What specific preparations does a chair person need to make prior to the start of a session?
2. How do you announce the opening of the session and introduce the presenters?
3. How do you manage the Q&A time?
4. What are the appropriate ways to say thank-you to the speakers and audience?
5. How do you mediate conflicts in the Q&A session as a presider in order to secure a smooth operation of the meeting?

The role of the chairperson is to ensure that the conference runs both smoothly and effectively according to the conference schedule. It is said that the job of chairing a session requires special skills and techniques. When everything works well, no one pays attention to the efforts made by the chair but when something goes wrong, everyone looks to the chair for a solution. In fact, the chairperson shoulders great responsibility, and even plays a decisive role for the success of the session.

In this unit, we are going to talk about how to chair a session and how to deal with some unexpected situations. As the moderator of the session, the presider is supposed to keep it moving according to a prescheduled arrangement. The chairperson will announce the beginning of the meeting, introduce the speakers and their topics, organize discussions, close the session, etc. All of these have to be done in a courteous and professional manner.

12.1 Preparations Before the Session

Classroom Voice

Sally is a PhD student. Her department organizes an international academic conference which involves scholars from different countries. The conference is to take place next month and she is designated as the chairperson of a parallel session because of her proficiency in English as well as in her research. Sally feels very proud of herself. In spite of feeling proud, she is also a bit nervous because she has never presided over an academic meeting in English. She wonders what necessary preparations should be made in order to make the session a success.

UNIT 12 Presiding over a Session

Instructor's Voice

The function of a session chair is to lead the session. As the leader, the chairperson must stay composed and needs to make necessary and detailed arrangements before the meeting takes place. The following are the activities a presider should perform beforehand in addition to the speeches for the meeting.

1) Check the Audiovisual Equipment

The chair has to arrive early to make sure that the audiovisual equipment, including the notebook computer, microphone, laser pointer and the timer, works well. Otherwise it could be extremely annoying and disturbing for the presenters and audience if the devices are not in a good condition. Understanding who to turn to when something unexpected takes place will be a great relief. So when some emergency happens, the chairperson can go or send volunteers for help. It is also advisable to load the chair's presentation on the laptop associated with the podium and try a sample speech. Remember to give some tips to the speakers on how to use the equipment properly when necessary.

2) Talk to the Speakers

Prior to the meeting, the chairperson may greet the presenters and help to relax them if they feel nervous. The chair is supposed to ask them to load their presentations on the common computer and have them run through the slides to check if everything, especially the movie and sound clips, works properly.

In addition, it is also the chairperson's responsibility to remind the speakers how the session will be organized. The chairperson should tell them how much time is allocated for the speeches, how much time will be allowed for queries and answers, and how to show them time is up (a card or a gesture is often preferred).

Another crucial issue is to know the exact pronunciation of every presenter's name. As the organizer of the session, the presider is supposed to double-check the meeting program to make sure who is going to present because it is not always the first author who delivers the speech. And if there is any confusion about how to pronounce a name, the chair can go to the speaker and ask for the right way to say it.

> Tasks

❶ Work out a checklist of the tasks that a chair needs to perform before the start of a parallel session.

❷ Are there any other pre-session preparations the chair should make to guarantee the session will run smoothly? Share your findings in a small group.

> Language Toolkit

Useful Expressions and Sentence Patterns of Chairing the Conference:

- to arrive at the conference venue/room ahead of time
- a remote control/projector/wireless microphone
- to arrange the conference room
- to make sure the participants sit face to face as much as possible
- to check if the batteries are overused,
- the conference program/schedule
- to bring the presentation to the session on a USB drive
- to load the presentation on the laptop
- to run through the slides
- to communicate with the audience
- to set the time limit and stick to it
- to circulate/distribute the handouts, agendas or other materials
- first/at the beginning
- next/then/after that/later/soon/shortly after
- finally/in the end/eventually/at last
- meanwhile/at the same time/concurrently/in the mean time
- …is essential/indispensable for…
- There ought to be…
- …is expected to…
- It would be good to…
- There are very few things that are more annoying than…

UNIT 12 Presiding over a Session

- …is needed in case…
- The chairperson should bear in mind that…

Reflection & Practice

1. Interview one of your classmates about the meetings or discussions they have presided over. It could be an experience of being a chairperson for a formal or informal gathering or a leader in group discussion in class. Try to find out answers to the following questions:

   1) How did he or she feel at that time?

   2) What preparations were made?

   3) Were they effective? Why or why not?

2. Suppose you are invited to be the chair of a seminar in the meeting room of your department building. Your mentor is going to be a speaker to share his/her latest achievements in research and all the graduate students in your department will attend it. Make a detailed list of the preparations you are going to make for the forthcoming event.

12.2 Making an Opening Speech and Introducing a Speaker

Classroom Voice

After deliberate preparation, it is finally the due time for Sally to start the parallel session. She is standing in the front of the meeting room as the chairperson. The audience has arrived and the presenters have been notified about the rules to follow. How will she get the attention of the attendees and introduce the speakers? Is she ready to introduce the speakers and highlight each one's achievements?

Instructor's Voice

As the attendees arrive individually at the venue, they need some time to settle themselves and get ready for the forthcoming activities. To make a transition, it is time to deliver a succinct speech. The presider should stand confidentially, speak slowly, make eye contact and sound positive. And the speech usually consists of two parts: (1) an opening speech; (2) introduction to the first speaker.

An opening address aims to attract the attention of the audience as well as set the scene for the meeting. And the introduction to the speaker offers explanation why this person was selected. The purpose is to show the credibility that he/she is qualified to talk about the specific topic to this audience.

12.2.1 Making an Opening Speech

An opening speech is delivered to announce the beginning of an occasion, such as a conference, seminar or parallel session. The audience and the situation should be highlighted in the speech. The aim is to greet the audience, explain why the meeting is so exciting and attractive, set the tone for the scheduled activities and tell the audience what to expect. The speech, therefore, is usually composed of two components: one is to welcome the audience and the other is to introduce the session.

In the first part, the chairperson greets the attendees at the beginning of the speech and welcomes them to the event. The chair steps to the front of the room to start promptly. He may need to tap the microphone gently to quiet the listeners and make a self-introduction and a concise welcoming speech.

Although the participants probably know where they are, it is still a good idea to mention the name of the event in the opening speech. It could be helpful to include information about the event's locale, for example the room number, in the speech as well.

When pronouncing the names, the chair needs to do so in a slow and clear way to make sure everyone can catch them. It is also one of the presider's duties to remind the audience to turn off or mute the cell phones.

In the second part, the chair is supposed to introduce the session to the audience. One of the major goals is to engage the listeners and arouse their interests. Therefore, it is preferred to show how the topics in the session are tied to each other and/or the importance of the topics. The chair can also pose a common question or a shared concern confronting the attendees. Besides, indicating the relevance between the following presentations and the issues the audience are facing now will attract them and keep them in the room.

In addition, the presider may as well inform the listeners the rules for the session, including the number of the speakers, how much time each speaker has and how much time is allocated for questions and answers. It helps to avoid confusion later on.

Finally, the chair may express hopes for the event, for example, wishing the attendees an enjoyable meeting or hoping that they will take away some thought-provoking information.

UNIT 12 Presiding over a Session

❯ Tasks

❶ Summarize the Does and Don'ts for a chair when he is delivering an opening speech. Can you think of any other tips besides the points mentioned in the text?

❷ Role-play. Suppose you are invited to be the chair of a seminar where your supervisor is going to be a speaker and all the graduate students in your department will attend it, make an opening address for the forthcoming event.

❯ Language Toolkit

1) Useful Expressions and Sentence Patterns of Calling for Attention

- Right, is everybody here? Good, I think we can start. Good morning, ladies and gentlemen, welcome to session (name or number) of the (name) conference. I am (your name) and will be your session chair.

- Good morning, friends and colleagues. May I have your attention please? I'd like to welcome you all on behalf of the department/Faculty/the organizers. I am…from… University/Department. It is a privilege/an honour for me to chair this session.

2) Useful Expressions and Sentence Patterns of Introducing the Theme and Program of the Meeting

- The theme of our meeting this afternoon is to review the development in…

- The purpose/aim of this session is to discuss the issue of…

- We are fortunate to have with us several dedicated and outspoken experts to share with us their latest findings regarding…There will be time at the end of the presentation for any questions you may have.

- You can see from the programme that we have a lot to get through today. I'd like to remind participants that they have a maximum of 10 minutes for their presentation with 10 minutes allocated for questions at the end.

12.2.2 Introducing a Speaker

Next, it is time to introduce the first speaker. A positive, confident introduction from the session chair builds up a desirable first-impression of the speaker. It not only arouses interest of the audience but also enhances confidence of the addresser. The chair is responsible to deliver a mini-speech to highlight the presenter's expertise by notifying the authors of the paper (if there are more than one), the presenter's name, affiliation, achievement, etc. The following offers some guidelines for the chair on how to introduce the guest speakers.

(1) Some research work is required. Even though the biography has already been provided by the speaker or the organizing committee, the chair is supposed to search online or talk to the speaker ahead of time. Type the name into a search engine and search for the details that relate to the speech. News articles, websites associated with the speaker or interviews could provide interesting information. What's more, try to contact the speaker if possible and ask how the person would like to be introduced.

(2) Find out what the speech is about. The chair may ask around for the focus of the presentation. What is more important is to point out why this topic should be timely and of interest to the audience. They can therefore be persuaded and engaged to listen to the speaker.

(3) To end the introduction, the chair usually welcomes the speaker to the podium by announcing the exact title of the presentation and saying his or her name again. When announcing the title of the presentation as well as the speaker's name, make sure to introduce precisely and with enthusiasm.

(4) One of the crucial rules of chairing is to always keep the podium occupied. The audience is likely to think the session is not well-organized or even out of control if the podium is left empty. Therefore the chairperson should remain at the front of the room until the presenter comes and gets ready to start. If the speaker is still busy loading the last-minute updates of the presentation, it is the chair's duty to fill the gap with more detailed introduction to the speaker or his/her research. Likewise, when the speaker departs, the chairperson is expected to meet him/her before he/she leaves and stay at the lectern until the next presenter has been introduced and is ready to talk.

Tasks

1 Summarize the guidelines on making introductions to the speakers for a session chair.

2 When referring to the biography of a scholar, you will find it covers a wide range of aspects including the titles, memberships, detailed research experience as well as the education background, even the paper title. It is proposed that achievement and relevance may serve as the guidelines on selecting the appropriate aspects from the chair's perspective. As far as you are concerned, how shall you choose the appropriate personal information about the speakers which is to be highlighted in the chair's introduction?

UNIT 12 Presiding over a Session

› Language Toolkit

1) Useful Expressions and Sentence Patterns of Introducing a Speaker

- Ladies and gentlemen, I'd like to welcome Professor/Doctor Wang/ Mr/Ms Wang, who will speak on… (**title + name + topic**)

- It is my pleasure to introduce our first speaker this morning, Professor/Doctor Wang/ Mr/Ms Wang. He/She is a well-known authority on…(**name + title + research area**)

- OK, now let's move on to the first speaker. I'm delighted to introduce Professor Wang from…University, who will tell us something about... (**title + name + affiliation + topic**)

- From 2016 to 2020, he was affiliated with (**name of a university/institution/ company**), (**name of the city**), (**country**).

- She is the (job title). Prior to this, she served as (job title)/served on (name of a university/institution/company). (**present and prior affiliation or title**)

- She has earned her doctoral degree in (subject) from (name of university). She also holds a Master's degree in (subject) from (name of the university) and is a bachelor graduate from (name of the university). (**educational background**)

- He has authored a number of influential books and journal papers, including… (**academic publications**)

- Dr. /Mr/Ms…has published extensively on the topic of…(**academic publications**)

- Our speaker is the author of…and co-author of….She also serves as the editor of… (**academic publications**)

Dr. …has been honored many awards, including…and…(**awards**)

He has earned the title of…(**awards**)

2) Useful Expressions and Sentence Patterns of Introducing the Topic of the Speech

The topic of today's speech is…

The title of his/her presentation is…

Dr. …will speak to/address you on…

His/Her presentation is entitled…

Today, he/she is going to convey a unique/an insightful understanding of…

3) Useful Expressions and Sentence Patterns of Asking the Speaker to Start the Presentation

Please join me in welcoming Dr…

Now I'd like to hand over to you, Professor…

Now, ladies and gentlemen, let's give a warm welcome to Dr. …

> **Reflection & Practice**

1. Let's continue with the seminar you are going to preside over where your supervisor is a speaker and your fellow students are to show up. What are you going to say to start the event? And what aspects will you inform the audience in the introduction to your mentor? Share your opening speech and introduction in class.

2. Read the following opening address at a plenary session and identify the following elements in it. Put the sentence numbers in the following table.

① Ladies and gentlemen, it is 8 o'clock now. ② Please be quiet, get seated and put your cell phones silent. ③ Good morning! ④ I am Wang Li from ABC University. ⑤ It is my privilege to chair Session 5— Machine Learning and Computer Vision Systems. ⑥ On behalf of the organizing committee, I extend the warmest welcome to all of you.

⑦ In this session, we are going to exchange the latest theoretical developments and practical applications in the research field. ⑧ We are fortunate to have with us 5 pioneering speakers today. ⑨ Each has 20 minutes for presentation, followed by a question and answer session around 10 minutes. ⑩ I hope everyone here will enjoy our session and have a fulfilled morning.

Elements	Sentence numbers
Settling the audience	
Welcoming/greeting the audience	
Self-introduction of the chair	
Session introduction	
Rules to follow	
Wishes	

12.3 Q&A Sessions and Thank-You Speeches

Classroom Voice

Chairing a meeting means more than announcing the start and end of it, and it is a complicated and demanding task which requires insightful observation, prompt coordination and tactful interpersonal skills. It is very likely that some unexpected situations will pop up during the meeting and they need to be handled properly, especially during the Q&A sessions.

The chair therefore needs to be fully prepared for the routines as well as the interruptions. How should Sally, the PhD student who takes the chair at the parallel meeting, manage the Q&A session? What will she say to notify a speaker that it is time to stop? What does she need to do if nobody poses a question to the speaker? And how could she extend her sincere appreciation to the speakers after their presentations?

Instructor's Voice

The function of a session chair is to lead the session—in the Q&A sessions, the chair is responsible to keep the session moving according to a pre-arranged schedule, in a courteous and professional manner.

Many academic conferences and events schedule the session as either part of a presentation or a stand-alone event. There are for sure advantages of doing the Q&A immediately at the end of each presentation compared with performing it after several presentations, because the audience is likely to forget their questions.

Q&A sessions offer audiences the opportunity to learn more about certain topics or even make contacts with high-profile experts that they would never have the chance. If planned well, the Q&A session can become the highlight for all the participants. However, it does take time to prepare a memorable Q&A event, and certain tips need to be handled to make the event run smoothly.

1) Time Management

Skilled chairs keep an eye on the time and stick to the agenda as much as possible.

(1) Letting the speakers finish their presentations on time is crucial to guarantee the built-in discussion time. The chair may choose a simple sign to show at the proper time. One side of the card reads "3 minutes to go" while the other says "Time is up". Hold it above the chest level in case the presenter will miss the sign. It is even highly recommended to put the card above the head. Or the chair may verbally remind the speakers by saying softly, "3 minutes to go" and "time is up". If the presenter keeps moving on over the time limit, the chair's standing up on the stage is a good sign that he should wrap up.

(2) Stopping the question raiser on certain occasions. The Q&A sessions are expected to run as a collaboration between the speaker and audience. If a question raiser has talked too long, cut him off with, "Okay, please let the speaker answer". If someone seems to have no intention of asking a question, or is just talking about his own work, the chair may ask, "Sorry, shall we get to the question?" Brevity is always valued and encouraged. It is also part of the chairperson's responsibility to keep reminding people of how many people want to ask a question and how little time there is.

But if there remains no time for further questions, the chair should at least comment on the already submitted questions so that the attendees feel appreciated and are willing to propose questions later.

2) Keeping a Queue

Keeping a queue is preferable over having everyone raise their hands after every response. Many people will stumble over their words when putting up their questions. It wastes the precious time when they keep saying "Oh, okay, well, um, in fact, so, I was thinking, uh…" The reason may lie in the fact that they haven't formulated their thoughts into a proper question yet. The ideal solution to improve the situation is not just to call on a person, but also say who will be up after that person. This allows sufficient preparation time for the question raisers, and they are almost always ready to raise their questions when called upon.

When determining an order, the chair should strive to make a queue of diversified identities or backgrounds, so that there are a variety of questions and perspectives. This involves mixing up senior and junior researchers, scholars at research institutions and scholars at teaching institutions, academics who work in the area and academics who don't, males and females, etc. It is suggested to arrange people who know the speaker well to the back of the line, because they may feel comfortable asking their questions on other occasions.

3) Preparing Ice-breaking Questions

It can take an audience some time to digest the content of a presentation and think of questions. Therefore, the session chair should always have one or two questions ready for the speaker. When there is silence and no question is proposed, the chairperson needs to break the ice. The question from the chair can be simple in order to relax the presenter and encourage the audience to go further and focus on some deeper or more specific questions. If possible, the chair may ask the presenter to provide a suggested question before the session starts if it is possible.

4) Applause

As the leader to the Q&A session, the chair also takes the lead to begin the applause. When the speakers are introduced, there usually goes no applause. However, there are three points that the chair is supposed to start the applause.

(1) End of the presentation. The presenter may say some closing words like "That's all for my presentation today. Thank you!". When he/she gives a clear signal that the presentation is ended, the chair should start the applause and the audience will join in.

(2) End of Q&A. When it is time to stop taking more questions, the chair should make some positive comments on the presentation and start a short round of applause and the

speaker can gather his/her material and leave the podium.

(3) End of the session. When the entire schedule is completed, the chair is supposed to express his/her gratitude for everyone for attendance and start another round of applause.

5) Thank-you Speeches

The speakers' willingness to share their time and expertise is crucial to the success of the event. A warm and meaningful post-speech thank-you will make the speakers feel appreciated while the audience will feel a sense of community.

The point is how to say thank-you in a sincere way while avoiding the clichés like "thanks for taking time out of your busy schedule". The key is to make it personal, specific and genuine. For personal remarks, the chair may need to talk to the speakers beforehand, chat for a while and listen intently for the points that might be mentioned to the audience. In addition, in order to make the speech specific, it is also advisable to highlight the most important elements referred to earlier in the presentations without copying directly from the presenter. Last but not least, the chair may as well condense the feedback into one or two adjectives that will liven the thank-you message and make it genuine.

Summarizing is also essential for a session and therefore should be included in the thank-you speech. It is effective to end a topic as well as to inform everyone what is going to take place next. The chairperson is expected to listen actively throughout the speeches and then produce impartial and concise summaries based on what was referred to earlier in a clear manner. It is an invaluable skill for a presider which will be perfected through practicing.

When it is time to close the meeting, the chair, as a rule, should end it with expressions of compliment, present a brief summary of the session, extends his/her appreciation to all the speakers and attendees as well as make a concise arrangement for the forthcoming activities.

› Tasks

❶ Summarize in your own words the tips for presiding over the Q&A session. You may follow the following outline.

1. Time Management
2. Keeping a Queue
3. Preparing Ice-breaking Questions
4. Thanking the Presenter
5. Being Enthusiastic

❷ Try to recall those impressive thank-you messages in formal occasions. Share them with your group members and discuss what elements have made them so distinct and unforgettable.

〉Language Toolkit

1) Useful Expressions and Sentence Patterns of Q&A Sessions & Time Management

- As we have several minutes for questions and comments, who would like to lead off?
- Do you have any questions for the speaker?
- Any questions? No. Well, it happens that I've got one.
- Mr. /Ms. …seems to have a question regarding the speech. Could you please share it with us?
- Anybody?
- Next question?
- Any other/additional questions/comments from the floor?
- Unfortunately, we have very limited time, and we must conclude so the next presenter/question can begin. Further questions can be addressed after the end of the session or outside the conference room.
- I'm sorry. Since we are already 10 minutes behind the schedule, would you continue your discussion after our session?
- Dr. …'s presentation has run over 10 minutes. There will be no discussion after this address.
- I think that's enough about…Can we now move on to the next speaker?
- I think we have covered the main points. Let's move on to the next presentation.

2) Useful Expressions and Sentence Patterns of Thank-you Message

- I'd like to extend my thanks to Dr…for sharing his thought-provoking talk regarding...
- Thanks for an excellent presentation, Dr. …
- Thank you for providing us with…
- Many thanks for addressing us on…It was an informative and inspiring speech.
- Thank you for helping us become more aware of the problems of…and the ways we can help solve them.
- We know how busy you are, so we are grateful that you would take the time to prepare and spend this morning/afternoon with us.

- I would like to thank again our speakers for their very interesting and stimulating contributions and the participants for the valuable following discussion.

3) Useful Expressions and Sentence Patterns of Summarizing

- So, can I just summarize what has been discussed so far?
- I'd now like to sum up the main points of our discussion.
- The audience is intrigued by…
- Dr. …has identified innovative ways to…
- The findings are interesting/informative and enlightening/illuminating.
- The talk is particularly appropriate at this time when we are considering…Many of us were especially interested in your analysis of…
- We look forward to implementing…
- We were previously unaware of…
- Before I finish, let me just say…

❯ Reflection and Practice

Think about the following questions before you practise:

1. If a speaker keeps droning on over his time limit, what shall you do to stick to the time limit as much as possible? Role-play the situation with one of your classmates, one playing the role of the droning speaker and the other being the chair.

2. If the question raisers have completely different viewpoints and keep arguing with the presenter, what should the chair do to moderate the dispute and run the Q&A session according to the agenda?

3. Suppose you are invited to be the chair of a seminar where your mentor is going to be a speaker to share his latest research breakthroughs and all the graduate students in your department will attend it, what ice-breaking questions will you ask and how will you manage the discussion session and offer your appreciation to the speaker's contribution to the meeting?

4. Read the closing speech, identify the following factors and put the sentence numbers in the table.

Element	Sentence number
Theme of the speech	
Briefly review the meeting	
Hope for the future	
Thank-you message	
Schedule a further meeting	

Ladies and gentlemen,

① In the closing session I would like to take this opportunity, on behalf of the Board of Directors of the ABC Association, to give the closing speech.

② This week we have covered so many important and complex problems in the field of XYZ. ③ The conference has been very fruitful. ④ Now we all have the same sense of passion and joy, and are reluctant to part, but the conference is drawing to a close.

⑤ It is our hope that the results of the conference will arouse the concern and interest of more and more researchers of all countries and will benefit all workers in the field of XXX. ⑥ We hope to keep close contact and cooperation with each other in the field of research work.

⑦ In bidding farewell to you all, I take this opportunity to request you to convey our profound friendship, our best regards and respect to your people.

⑧ As the General Secretary of the conference, and on behalf of the Board of Directors, I would like to express our sincere thanks to the members of the International Committee, and the members of Organizing Committee. ⑨ Thanks are also due to those who made contributions to its success, and of course, to all of you who have come from so far away.

⑩ Let's meet again in Science City next year.

Unit 13
Co-constructing a Simulated International Conference

Learning Objectives

- To understand the detailed preparation of international conferences;

- To be familiar with the procedure of international academic conferences;

- To obtain essential skills required by simulating international academic communication.

Pre-learning Questions

1. Why do you need to hold a simulated international conference?
2. How do you co-construct a simulated international conference by students and the teacher?

In this unit, you are going to learn how to co-construct a simulated international conference. Clarifying the significance of simulating international conference comes first, followed by becoming familiar with the procedure. To ensure the success of simulating international conference, establishing the preparatory committees will be the priority.

13.1 The Significance of Co-constructing a Simulated International Conference

Classroom Voice

As a first-year graduate student, Emily has already done a lot of experiments in laboratory. But she is still unconfident about her scientific research and has no idea about how to communicate with foreign scholars fluently and academically. Self-consciousness controls her all the time. What she could do in her research field is a puzzle that still haunts her.

Instructor's Voice

International conference, a large scale of official gathering of professionals coming from every corners of the world, either face-to-face or via Internet or satellite, usually lasting for a few days, is a kind of communication platform where people with the same work or interests come together to discuss their views or findings.

For graduate students, research beginners, international conferences are the best way for them to present and discuss their ideas and findings, particularly for those graduates who hope their research will be improved into a higher level.

However, self-confidence in communication with foreign colleagues is built up day by day through long-term practices. And it also needs huge bravery to join in an international academic conference as a green hand. Practice makes perfect. At the end of this course, it is of significance for graduate students to construct a simulated academic conference with the help of the instructor. Co-constructing a simulated international academic conference cannot only examine the teaching and learning results, but also drive the students to apply what they have learned from this course and to develop their teamwork spirit and collaboration awareness. Firstly, it is necessary to examine whether the students are able to distinguish the varieties of international conferences and to be clear about how a real international conference is organized and constructed.

13.1.1 Distinguishing the Varieties of International Conferences

> **Task**

Discuss with your partner about the varieties of international conferences: What are they? What are the differences? How to distinguish them? Get your own answer to the questions above and then continue the discussion with your teammates by filling in the table below and make a presentation as your group findings.

Varieties	Definitions	Examples	Remarks
Meeting	A situation in which two or more people meet together.		
Conference	A large official meeting, usually lasting for a few days, at which people with the same work or interests come together to discuss their views.		
Symposium	A meeting at which experts have discussion about a particular subject.		
Congress	A large formal meeting or series of meetings where representatives from different groups discuss ideas, make decisions.		
Convention	A large meeting of the member of a profession, a political party held at regular intervals.		
Forum	A meeting organized for people that can exchange opinions and ideas on a particular issue.		

(cont.)

Varieties	Definitions	Examples	Remarks
Seminar	A class at university or college when a small group of students and a teacher discuss or study a particular topic.		
Workshop	A period of discussion and practical work on a particular subject, in which a group of people share their knowledge and experience.		

13.1.2 Mastering the Whole Procedures of International Conferences

After distinguishing the varieties of international conference, you will be clear about the distinctive characteristics of a wide range of international academic conferences. Learning from the real international conferences can facilitate students to have a clear idea about the blueprint of the simulated international academic conference.

> Tasks

Make an analysis about international academic conferences in your disciplines in terms of conference information components, names, websites, major activities, and make a research report following the table below and discuss about your findings with your group members.

Conference name	Information component	Website	Major activities

UNIT 13 Co-constructing a Simulated International Conference

(cont.)

Conference name	Information component	Website	Major activities

13.2 Major Sessions of Simulated International Conferences

Classroom Voice

Emily has realized she needs to participate in an international conference to examine her academic research findings. Preparing her paper is just one thing of the whole preparation. There are still a lot of other information for her to grasp. She needs a practice by participating in simulated international conferences.

Instructor's Voice

An international conference is a significant way for professionals, academics and those researchers with a common interest, including graduate students who are pursuing their master or doctor degrees, to get together and exchange their ideas, especially those most cutting-edges ones in their field.

In order to co-conduct a simulated international conference well, you need to know the basic organization of an international conference.

13.2.1 Organization of an International Conference

Basically speaking, an organization of an international conference includes the following parties:

1) Sponsors and Organizers

It's said that the sponsor is the one or the institution which can initiate and finance the international conference, which also have the right to nominate the organizers they trust in.

2) General Chairman

General Chairman is the one in control, directing in work committees and coordinating with subcommittee, which ensure smooth take-place of this international conference.

3) General Secretary

General Secretary, regarded as General Chairmen's right-hand man, handles daily routines of this international conference, including reporting to the committee every day, charging the finical management, and arranging conferences activities.

4) Academic Committee

Academic Committee is served as an advisory body taking charge of the chief academic policy, which distinguishes this international academic conference from a general one. Their routine work includes designing the agenda, arranging academic communication, collecting and evaluating the papers they've received.

13.2.2 Routine Work of Organizing an International Conference

> **Task**

Now you have got basic idea about the organization of an international academic conference. Talk with your teammates and make a group decision to set up an organization of your own simulated international academic conferences and fill the following table.

	Name	Routine work 1	Routine work 2	Routine work 3	Routine work 4	Comment
Sponsors						
Organizers						

UNIT 13 Co-constructing a Simulated International Conference

(cont.)

	Name	Routine work 1	Routine work 2	Routine work 3	Routine work 4	Comment
General Chairman						
General Secretary						
Academic Committee						

13.3 How to Co-construct a Simulated International Conference

Classroom Voice

Now Emily faces a job to construct a simulated international conference. It's the first time for Emily to organize such a large event. What she thinks she should do at the beginning is that she needs to call for a group of volunteers. Are anything else on the to-do list? She is puzzled and in a great confusion.

Instructor's Voice

Recently, most of the graduates have realized that if they want to make a successful simulated international conference, it is essential that they should establish a website, social media channels and even personal contacts to promote their conference. A preparatory committee for it is absolutely needed.

An international academic conference must include but not limited by those below:

- Name of the international conference

  Each international conference need a formal name, which can be short for easily remembering but clearly summarize the theme of the conference.

- Theme

  Theme is the subject or the main idea of the international conference.

- Objectives

  Objectives are the target that the international conferences want to get.

- Date/Location

  Date and location is the basic information that an international conference notice must have, for the starting and ending date and the place it will be held.

- Requirements for attendance

  An international conference notice may give some specific requirement to the conference participants, as membership, age or some specialization.

- Call for abstracts

  Submitting abstracts is the way for the academic committee to decide whether a participant has a right or not to attend the international conference.

- Conference sponsors/organizer/committee

  It's an organization for the participants to know.

- Registration

  Registration for the meeting must be made to known to all participants of the international conference.

- Accommodation/Contact information

  Accommodation and contact information is also information that must be shown to all about the international conferences.

13.3.1 To-do list at the Very Beginning of a Simulated International Conference

> Task

Discuss those questions with your teammates to fill the tables as follows:

If you want to construct an international conference, what is the steps you will take?
1.
2.
3.
4.

Write down those things that might promote your simulated academic conferences:
1.
2.

| 3. |
| 4. |

13.3.2 Promoting a Simulated International Conference

When you determine to construct a simulated international conference, it is imperative for you to formulate the working scheme to promote its advance as planned. Although you may have no experience of attending any international conference for that matter, so far you have learned everything about it and the instructor has equipped your with the basic skills throughout the whole course for the simulated conference.

It's not enough to only name your conference and expect people to attend. What you need to think carefully is how you attract the right persons that your conference involves. International conferences also need the marketing and advertising. Maybe someone will notice the conference when it makes a call for paper, but a concerted second push like making an exclusive website for the conference and writing an attractive notice to announce the theme of the conference will absolutely increase the number of registrations.

> Tasks

❶ This is a screenshot of the website—allconferencealert.net, which includes many famous international conference, especially the academic one. In this task, you are allowed to analyze this screenshot below carefully and tell your partner the detailed information you have noticed from it. And check it on Internet and make revision of your answers connected with Task 4.

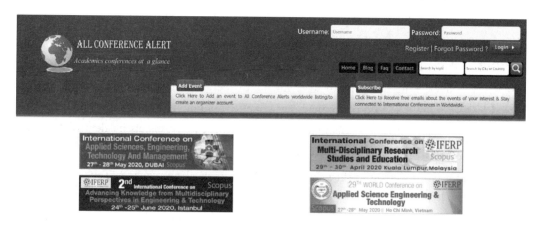

Figure 13.1 The Screenshot of the Website—all conferencealert.net

❷ **Name your simulated international conference with your teammates and make a notice of it following the sample below.**

About ICASETM

The International Conference on Applied Sciences, Engineering, Technology and Management (ICASETM-20), which is scheduled to take place on the 27th and 28th of May, 2020 in the beautiful city of Dubai will focus on establishing the bar for effective future inclinations with engineering, applied sciences, technology, and management. The international conference has been specifically designed with the intention of delivering outstanding outcomes and challenges in the engineering sector. It intends to bring collectively researchers, scientists, technicians and scholars in all fields of the applied sciences, engineering, technology, and management, for the propagation of original research conclusions, new approaches and developmental practices that yield real results.

Participants will be afforded the incredible chance to interact with leading experts from their respective fields, taking the opportunity to draw everyone commonly in a panel and to bestow their plans in different countries.

ICASETM-20 strives to join the gap among researchers and academics in various domains, and this type of long-term imagination has resulted in the launching of this incredible and unique initiative involving experts from all fields. ICASETM-20 is organized specially to furnish delegates with hard-to-find knowledge and expertise that they will find nowhere else.

Conference Objectives

The main objective of the International Conference on Applied Sciences, Engineering, Technology and Management (ICASETM-20) is to encourage scientific and informative exercises for the development of participants' lives by promoting the theory and application of different disciplines and divisions linked to the hurdles of experimental research.

One of the goals of ICASETM-20 is to give specialists a world-class stage to distribute research discoveries by using innovative means of lecturing and presenting. This one-of-a-kind lecture output will be of tremendous benefit to students participating in the event. Scientists will also be invited to distinguish significant research subjects in identified regions in the fields of applied sciences, engineering, technology, and management.

The International Conference On Applied Sciences, Engineering, Technology And Management (ICASETM-20), one of the most comprehensive professional conferences of its kind in world, has been specifically designed to present technical and other assistance to intensify research and development enterprises, by proclaiming high quality research findings, as well as research papers/articles.

UNIT 13 Co-constructing a Simulated International Conference

13.3.3 Calling for Papers of a Simulated International Conference

If you want to make submission to an international conference, you should follow some requirements of it:

- make a detailed title of your submission, including title of the submission, with clear topic area and presentation format;
- write two or three sentences to describe your presentation prepared beforehand;
- notice clearly authors information, with full name, department, university and e-mail address;
- e-mail your abstract or paper.

> Task

Most international conferences have their own websites to promote conferences. The two pictures below are both aimed at calling for papers. Look at the screenshot carefully and find useful information you need and then share it with your teammates.

Figure 13.2   Call for Papers of Research Society

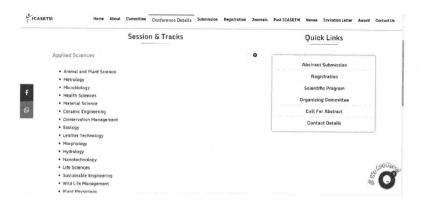

Figure 13.3   Call for Papers of ICASETM

13.3.4 Invitation Letter of a Simulated International Conference

After preparing conference notice and preparing calling for papers, the simulated international conference is on the way. Now it's time for you to prepare the invitation letter.

> Task

Look at the Figure 13.4 as follows, discuss with your partner and make your own invitation letters.

Figure 13.4 Invitation Letter of ICMDRSE

13.3.5 Agenda of a Simulated International Conference

> Task

Look at the agenda carefully, and learn the process you will do during the conference day. And then make your own agenda about your simulated international conference with your team members.

Program Agenda

Time	Session
8:30 AM - 9:00 AM	Registration
9:00 AM - 9:10 AM	Opening Ceremony
9:10 AM - 9:20 AM	Speech By IFERP Director
9:20 AM - 9:30 AM	Group Photo
9:30 AM - 9:45 AM	Coffee Break

UNIT 13 Co-constructing a Simulated International Conference

(cont.)

Time	Session
9:45 AM - 10:00 AM	Keynote Speeches
10:00 AM - 1:00PM	Technical Presentation Session
1:00 PM - 2:00PM	Lunch Break
2:00 PM - 3:45PM	Technical Presentation Session
3:45 PM - 4:00PM	Coffee Break
4:00 PM - 5:00PM	Technical Presentation Session
5:00 PM - 5:10PM	Ending Ceremony

Agenda of Your Simulated International Conference

Time	Session

13.4 The Evaluation of a Simulated International Conference

Classroom Voice

All those above is the preparation for the simulated international conference, and then the day is coming. Emily is so nervous to think about the details during the time when the conference is around the corner. As the host of this simulated international conference, it's a magnificent challenge for her in her graduate study, as well as for her teammates.

Instructor's Voice

This is the most comprehensive practice for graduates' academic English communication ability, a practice for a simulated conference based on specific abilities trained in each unit. But, it should be emphasized that unlike a real international conference, the simulated parallel sessions cannot be arranged simultaneously in so many separate conference rooms. However, it is still a wonderful choice to train students and develop their confidence in future academic career.

Tasks

In this task, the whole class are asked to prepare a simulated international conference. Perform tasks: make an organization, determine the theme of the organization, write the international conference notice, call for papers, and send invitation letters or other correspondence, and apply for a website if necessary.

Name of your simulated international conference

UNIT 13 Co-constructing a Simulated International Conference

Website screenshot if you have

Announcement of your simulated international conference

Calling for papers and invitation letters of your simulated international conference

Agenda of that day

❯ Reflection & Practice

1. After learning this unit, could you conduct a simulated international conference with your teammates? Which kind of jobs will you choose to do, an organizer, a host, a participator or others?

2. If you have a chance to give an evaluation to your performance in the simulated international conference, how could you evaluate it?

3. It's said that it's a final training of your academic English communication ability in your graduate study. In retrospect, what have you acquired?

References

Aguisando, M. D. 2014. Academic self-concept and the English competencies among English learners in the University of the Immaculate Conception. *UIC Research Journal*, *20*(1).

Anderson, K., Maclean, J., & Lynch, T. 2004. *Study Speaking: A Course in Spoken English for Academic Purposes.* 2nd ed. Cambridge: Cambridge University Press.

Bailey, S. 2001. *Academic Writing: A Handbook for International Students.* 3rd ed. Oxford: Routledge.

Bateman, A. & Bourne, P. E. 2009. Ten simple rules for chairing a scientific session. *PLoS Computational Biology*, *5*(9): e1000517.

Beel, J. 2014. Comprehensive comparison of reference managers: Mendeley vs. Zotero vs. Docear. 01-15. From ISG Siegen website.

Blaj-Ward, L. 2017. *Language Learning and Use in English-Medium Higher Education.* Cham: Palgrave Macmillan.

Brown, G. & Yule, G. 1984. *Teaching the Spoken Language.* Cambridge: Cambridge University Press.

Carlock, J., Eberhardt, M., Horst, J., & Menasche, L. 2017. *The ESL Writer's Handbook.* Ann Arbor: University of Michigan Press.

Chris, W. & Joana, O. 2019. When English is not your mother tongue. *Nature, 570*: 265-267.

Coley, W. & Law, J. 2015. *Research Paper.* 16th ed. Beijing: Beijing Language and Culture University Press.

Habas, C. 2019. How to preside over a meeting. 06-01. From bizfluent website.

Harmon, I. 2019. How to prepare for a poster session. 09-12. From West Virginia University Libraries website.

Harvey, S. 2017. Book review on researching contexts, practices and pedagogues in English for academic purposes. *Journal of English for Academic Purposes*, *28*: 51-54.

Isidore, C. 2020. Falling sales, job losses and bankruptcies: Pain spreads across coal country. 12-09. From CNN website.

Jennings, C. A. 2019. Ten tips for presiding officers (per Robert's rules). From Dummies website.

Jordan, R. R. 1997. *English for Academic Purposes*. Cambridge: Cambridge University Press.

Kittler, M. 2018. Do we understand each other? Discussing academic exchange from a cross-cultural communication perspective. *International Studies of Management & Organization, 48*(3): 333-351.

Kowasch, M. 2018. Nickel mining in northern New Caledonia—a path to sustainable development?. *Journal of Geochemical Exploration, 194*(11): 280-290.

Langan, J. 2004. *College Writing Skills with Readings*. 5th ed. Beijing: Foreign Language Teaching and Research Press.

Larkins, K. 2019. Tips for chairing meetings. From KSL Training website.

Ma, Y. 2018. Ma Yun's speech in the commencement ceremony of Hong Kong University. From haokan website.

Madduxb. 2017. Types of conferences. 04-14. From OSU website.

Mandalios, J. 2013. RADAR: An approach for helping students evaluate Internet sources. *Journal of Information Science, 39*: 470-478.

Markus, K. 2018. Do we understand each other? Discussing academic exchange from a cross-cultural communication perspective. *International Studies of Management & Organization, 48*(3): 333-351.

McCurry, D. 2019. A complete guide to academic conferences. From Ex Ordo website.

Mewburn, I. 2010. Five top ways to better academic networking. 09-23. From Thesis Whisperer website.

National Education Examinations Authority. 2018. China's standards of English language ability. From NEEA website.

Otero-Iglesias, M. 2017. The great benefits of attending academic conferences. From UACES website.

Selinker, L., Taarone, E., & Hanzeli, V. 1981. *English for Academic and Technical Purposes*. Rowley: Newburg House.

Spencer, C. M. & Arbon, B. 1996. *Foundations of Writing: Developing Research and Academic Writing*. Illinois: National Textbook Company.

Steer, J. 1995. *Strategies for Academic Communication*. Boston: Heinle & Heinle Publishers.

WhatisResearch. 2018. How to find academic conferences. 10-11. From WhatisResearch website.

Wisker, G. 2018. *The Postgraduate Research Handbook*. 2nd ed. Shanghai: Shanghai Foreign Language Education Press.

蔡基刚. 2015. 通用学术英语. 上海：复旦大学出版社.

陈美华. 2011. 学术英语口语教程. 南京：南京大学出版社.

陈美华. 2013. 学术英语交流. 北京：外语教学与研究出版社.

从丛，王文宇. 2014. 学术交流英语教程. 第2版. 北京：外语教学与研究出版社.

范娜. 2019. 国际学术交流英语. 北京：清华大学出版社.

郭月琴，武学峰，郑琳. 2017. 国际学术交流英语教程. 北京：中国人民大学出版社.

洪卫. 2012. 学术交际英语. 北京：电子工业出版社.

胡庚申. 2000. 国际学术交流英语. 北京：高等教育出版社.

胡庚申. 2001. 论文写作与发表. 北京：高等教育出版社.

胡庚申. 2017. 国际会议交流. 北京：外语教学与研究出版社.

胡庚申，申云祯，范红. 2000. 国际会议交流英语. 北京：高等教育出版社.

贾卫国. 2008. 国际学术交流英语. 北京：外语教学与研究出版社.

姜怡，姜欣. 2015. 学术交流英语. 北京：高等教育出版社.

李琼花. 2019. 通用学术交流英语. 厦门：厦门大学出版社.

王芳. 2015. 学术交流英语. 西安：西安交通大学出版社.

王慧莉，刘文宇. 2015. 国际学术会议英语. 北京：中国人民大学出版社.

王松，顾晓乐. 2018. 国际学术交流英语. 北京：经济科学出版社.

吴岑. 2014. 国际学术交流英语教程. 南京：南京大学出版社.

杨晋. 2014. 研究生学术英语口语教程. 南京：南京大学出版社.

叶云屏. 2016. 理工专业通用学术英语. 北京：北京理工大学出版社.

张兢田，郭强. 2015. 学术英语口语教程. 上海：同济大学出版社.